RACIAL DISCRIMINATION
AND PRIVATE EDUCATION

RACIAL DISCRIMINATION AND PRIVATE EDUCATION

· *A LEGAL ANALYSIS* ·

By

Arthur S. Miller

CHAPEL HILL

The University of North Carolina Press

Copyright, 1957, by the Minnesota Law Review

Copyright, 1957, by The University of North Carolina Press

To Dagmar

INTRODUCTION

THE RELATIONSHIPS of ethnic groups—in broad terms, the relationship between the dark-skinned peoples and the whites, the Negroes, Mexicans, and Puerto Ricans and the remainder of the nation—is by far the most pressing social problem facing the United States today. The twentieth-century battle for the social-service state has in large part been won. Not won—perhaps the battle is not even fully joined as yet—is the place that the nonwhite will have in the American version of the welfare state. Brought to a sharp point by the Supreme Court decision in May, 1954, in the *Segregation Cases*, the attention of the nation is now riveted upon the pull-and-tug of opposing forces in the Negro's striving for an improved status. More, the remainder of the world is watching to see how the United States handles its most important domestic social problem.

This study of the legal problems involved in the racial desegregation of denominational and other private schools was undertaken in an attempt to fill, in part at least, a gap in the literature of racial relations in education. For the most part the attention of writers has recently been centered upon the public schools—justifiably so, for it is there that the problem is most intense and the contest bitterest. Nevertheless, the nonpublic school occupies an important place in American education, and it has problems similar to those that have plagued many public school administrators since May, 1954. The problems are, however, sufficiently different to merit separate development.

It has been my intention to raise and discuss the main problem areas involved in racial integration of private schools, but not to make an exhaustive listing of all the statutes and court decisions that could possibly bear upon the over-all question. The fluid nature of present-day racial relations soon makes any attempted exhaustive development out-of-date almost before publication. I have tried, thus, to be comprehensive—to touch upon the important questions that can be raised and to indicate the principal avenues that lead to an understanding of the problem area.

The study itself is chiefly focused upon the legal ramifications involved in any attempt by a private school to commingle the children of different skin color in its student body. In order, however, to get a proper perspective upon those aspects, I have sought to indicate briefly the position the private school has in the American system of education and to devote some time to certain nonlegal sanctions that might be invoked against an integrating private school. Originally, my intention was to look into only the question of what sanctions might be invoked against an integrating denominational school by a state government. But it soon proved to be advisable to broaden the scope to include all private schools and to discuss, in addition to nongovernmental sanctions, certain other relevant legal questions.

I should like, finally, to point out clearly that this study has nothing to do with the so-called "private school" plans which some Southern states have devised as a means of avoiding having to integrate their public schools. The study deals with true private education, not the ersatz variety.

Arthur S. Miller

Emory University, Georgia
August 1956

ACKNOWLEDGMENT

Part of the work on this study was made possible through a grant from the Fund for the Republic. The statements made, the conclusions drawn, the point-of-view expressed are, however, solely those of the author.

CONTENTS

Introduction — vii

I. The Private School System in America — 3

II. Governmental Sanctions against Integration — 21

III. Private Sanctions against Integration — 51

IV. The Public Nature of Private Education — 68

V. Limitations in Grants and Gifts — 97

VI. An Appraisal — 123

Table of Cases — 133

Index — 135

RACIAL DISCRIMINATION
AND PRIVATE EDUCATION

CHAPTER ONE

THE PRIVATE SCHOOL SYSTEM IN AMERICA

LARGELY NEGLECTED in the swirl of controversy that has developed since the May 17, 1954, decision of the Supreme Court in the *Segregation Cases*[1] is the private school and its position in the pattern of educational racial discrimination. Attention has been focused almost exclusively upon the public school systems and their administration, and, to a lesser extent, upon the announced plans of some states to establish a subsidized system of private schools as a means of avoiding the impact of the segregation decision. But the privately operated school in the southeastern United States, whether denominational or otherwise, has not escaped difficulty; it has not been able to avoid dealing with the same type of problems besetting the public school administrator. The specific manner in which the problems have arisen may differ but the broad pattern is basically similar. These difficulties, revolving around the admission practices of the nonpublic school, are both complex and important; they merit comprehensive

1. Brown v. Board of Education, 347 U.S. 483 (1954); Bolling v. Sharpe, 347 U.S. 497 (1954). Of the many discussions of these cases, both in and out of legal periodicals, the following is recommended for an up-to-date study of what has transpired since the decisions were rendered: McKay, " 'With All Deliberate Speed': A Study of School Desegregation," 31 *New York University Law Review* 991 (1956).

development and exposition. It is my purpose here to attempt such a development and exposition; particular emphasis will be placed upon the legal problems that are involved.

Required first of all is a preliminary inquiry into the social and legal context in which the private school administrator operates. What place does the private school occupy in American education today? What is the legal status of the private school? It is to these questions that our attention will first be directed. The discussion will be concerned with the bona fide private school as it has been known and not with the so-called private school plans announced by some Southern government officials during the past two years.[2] The term "private school" will be used generically to indicate both the denominational (parochial) school and the nonsectarian school.

THE PLACE OF NONPUBLIC EDUCATION

Private, i.e., nonpublic, education has long held an important place in the scheme of American education. This is particularly true of higher education: the private colleges and universities have always enrolled a high percentage, usually a majority, of the nation's youth who have gone on beyond high school. And it is also true of elementary and secondary education, although here the public schools have for many years educated a much greater number. With education itself considered a matter of

---

2. Some preliminary discussions of these plans have appeared. See, for example, Murphy, "Can Public Schools Be 'Private'?," 7 *Alabama Law Review* 48 (1954); Nicholson, "The Legal Standing of the South's School Resistance Proposals," 7 *South Carolina Law Quarterly* 1 (1954); Murphy, "Desegregation in Public Education—A Generation of Future Litigation," 15 *Maryland Law Review* 221 (1955); Paul, *The School Segregation Decision* (1954).

vital societal importance, perhaps crucial to the survival of the democratic system, the private schools have ably performed significant functions. The belief structure of the American people includes the notion that education has importance beyond the individual being educated—the public weal itself is considered to be dependent upon education conducted upon the broadest possible base. Disagreement with education is only over the details: *how* it is to be accomplished, not *if* it is. As the late Senator Robert Taft once remarked, we have "socialized education" in this country.

This is, it should be remembered, a belief relatively new in history. Universal education, like universal suffrage, is apparently a creature of the new world, and one that came rather late even there.[3] It exists, so the theory goes, to promote the general intelligence of the people and thus to increase their usefulness and efficiency. The aim is to provide a reasonably adequate grasp of the relevant facts important in the making of societal decisions together with a reasonably adequate training in thinking about and evaluating those facts.[4] The American people have consistently believed (with a minor exception no longer of consequence) that the ends to be achieved by mass education could be accomplished through the medium of school

---

3. General discussions of education, its history and development may be found in the encyclopedia. See, for example, 3 *Encyclopedia of the Social Sciences* 403 et seq. (1931). See also Carr, "The Federal Government and National Interest in Education," in Russell (editor), *National Policies for Education, Health and Social Services* 3 (1955).

4. Whether the theoretical justifications of some of the beliefs in mass education, particularly with regard to those dealing with asserted abilities of all people to make wise political decisions, can withstand rigorous analysis is questionable, but beyond the scope of the present study. Compare Lippmann, *The Public Philosophy* (1955) with Dahl, *A Preface to Democratic Theory* (1956).

systems both publicly and privately controlled. However, as will be shown below, the people generally have reserved the right to insure that private schools maintain standards similar to those established for the public schools. This right has not always been exercised; nevertheless, it is available for use should the need arise.[5]

Statistically, of course, the public school today greatly overwhelms the nonpublic. Of the 163,673 schools in existence in the academic year 1951-52 only 15,316 were private. Of this total, there were 10,666 elementary schools, 3,322 secondary schools, 137 residential schools for exceptional children, and 1,191 higher educational schools controlled privately. Compare these figures with those of the public schools for the same year: 123,763 elementary schools, 23,746 secondary, 307 residential for exceptional children, and 641 colleges and universities. Only in the higher educational bracket does the private school outnumber the public.

The same ratio holds true for enrollment. Out of a total school enrollment of 32,934,748 in 1951-52, about 15 percent (4,994,116) of the students attended private schools. This figure breaks down in this manner: about 13 percent (3,168,822 out of a total of 23,958,113) at the elementary level, 10 percent (678,967 out of a total of 6,596,351) at the secondary level, and 50 percent (1,146,327 out of a total of 2,380,284) in higher educa-

[5]. See National Education Association, *State Authority With Respect to the Establishment and Supervision of Nonpublic Schools and Colleges* (August, 1951); McLaughlin, *A History of State Legislation Affecting Private Elementary and Secondary Schools in the United States, 1870-1945* (1946); Note, 4 *Intramural Law Review of New York University* 35 (1948).

tion.[6] It is of particular interest to note a significant increase in private school enrollment, both absolutely and in comparison with the public schools, since the academic year of 1939-40. At that time 25,433,542 pupils were enrolled in public elementary and secondary schools and 2,611,047 in private schools—roughly one student in a private school to nine in the public schools. The figures for 1951-52 are 26,706,675 and 3,847,789—about one to seven. In 1955-56 it is estimated that the figures are 32,026,000 and 4,469,900—again, about one to seven. In absolute figures, elementary and secondary private school enrollments since 1939-40 have increased about 1,858,900 or nearly 71 percent, while public school enrollments have increased about 6,592,000 or nearly 26 percent. Thus, although the public school still greatly overshadows the private school quantitatively, the clear trend at the elementary and secondary school level is toward greater use by parents of the nonpublic school. As noted above, the private school already is used by more students than the public at the level of higher education. While the trend is clear, the reasons for this change are not so readily apparent and are probably multiple rather than single. Increased prosperity among people generally would allow more parents to send their children to the private school; also, the disquietude with the educational standards of many public schools, which is evident among many people, would tend to explain some of the increase in enrollment of the private schools. It is yet too early to determine whether racial

6. Statistical data in these paragraphs are taken from U.S. Department of Health, Education and Welfare, *Statistical Summary of Education, 1951-52* (1955). See Swanson and Griffin, *Public Education in the South* (1955).

integration since the Supreme Court's decision will cause any significant exodus from the newly-desegregated public schools to the private schools.[7]

In the sixteen states and District of Columbia which can be considered as making up the South, there are 53,568 public schools (43,259 elementary, 9,971 secondary, 115 for exceptional children, and 223 colleges and universities) and 2,950 private schools (1,786 elementary, 766 secondary, 22 for exceptional children, and 376 colleges and universities). Comparative enrollment statistics for Southern schools were unobtainable.

One other statistic is of interest: income in the academic year of 1951-52 was $11.7 billion for all schools, public and private and at all levels. Of this figure, $9.3 billion (79 percent) went to the public school systems, and $2.4 billion (21 percent) to the private. Thus, 21 percent of school income went to educate 15 percent of the nation's students. To the extent that monetary expenditures reflect a higher quality of education, the student at the private school is getting more and better education than the public school pupil.

THE LEGAL STATUS OF NONPUBLIC EDUCATION

Relatively rare, but nevertheless important, have been the cases decided by the United States Supreme Court in the field of education.[8] A handful have dealt with the admission practices of public schools; in another few the

---

7. It has been reported, however, that desegregation has caused a number of parents in the District of Columbia either to move their residences outside the District or to send their children to an available private school.

8. The cases are collected and discussed in Spurlock, *Education and the Supreme Court* (1955) (listing thirty-nine).

Court has made pronouncements on the relationship of religion to the public school systems; and there have been other educational matters that have raised questions relating to the federal Constitution. Similarly, Congress has made but few interventions in education, and these have been in aid of local education rather than attempts to control the details of educational administration. It can be said that the educational system has, by and large, satisfied national, as distinguished from purely local, requirements. If not, substantial federal intervention would undoubtedly have taken place long ago. One of the reasons for the current increased congressional concern in education, manifested in the proposed massive school building program, is the belief that national ends are not being achieved under the present system. The shortage of engineers and other technicians is one item of this federal concern, the belief being that our national security is imperiled by such a shortage.

Because of the lack of substantial federal intervention in education, a comprehensive inquiry into the legal status of private education must, perforce, be directed for the most part to state statutes and state court decisions. The United States Supreme Court has made only two decisions of any real importance to private schools: *Pierce v. Society of Sisters*[9] and *Meyer v. Nebraska*.[10] Of the two the *Pierce* case is probably the more significant. Since it was rendered in 1925 it is clear that parents may fulfill a state's educational requirements without use of the public school system. In other words, the right to send children to private schools was given constitutional protection.

9. 268 U.S. 510 (1925).
10. 262 U.S. 390 (1923).

Little else is settled regarding the extent of state authority over the nonpublic school. That the state may exercise some control is clear. However, the line between permissible control and that which is proscribed constitutionally has not yet been drawn. This lack of settlement may be traced, in part at least, to the fundamental disagreement over the theory of child control. The difference of opinion has its roots in antiquity; it can be traced at least as far back as Platonic times. The relevant question is this: Who, parent or state, has primary power over the education of the child? The question receives differing answers. While there are isolated judicial statements to the contrary, in addition to a great deal of opinion from church groups (chiefly Roman Catholic), it has been generally held by American courts that the state, not the parents, is pre-eminent. From this basic view courts have adhered to the position that the wishes of society, operating through the state governments, can control in basic educational matters even in those situations where the parents are in direct opposition. This, and the reasons for it, were succinctly put by the Supreme Court of New Hampshire:

> The primary purpose of the maintenance of the common school system is the promotion of the general intelligence of the people constituting the body politic and thereby to increase the usefulness and efficiency of the citizens, upon which the government of society depends. Free schooling furnished by the state is not so much a right granted to pupils as a duty imposed upon them for the public good. If they do not voluntarily attend the schools provided for them, they may be compelled to do so. While most people regard the public schools as the means of great personal advantage to the pupils, the fact is too often overlooked that they

are governmental means of protecting the state from the consequences of an ignorant and incompetent citizenship.[11]

But even so, as the *Pierce* case demonstrates, the state may not require attendance at public schools if parents wish to send their children to private schools. The state may not, in other words, legislate the private school out of existence. The language used by Mr. Justice McReynolds in *Pierce* bears striking resemblance to that of religious organizations, and illustrates, when compared to the New Hampshire case the conflict in basic theory. In an opinion that invalidated, because it was considered to be violative of due process of law, an Oregon statute requiring children of the ages of eight to sixteen to attend public schools, Justice McReynolds said:

> We think it entirely plain that the Act of 1922 unreasonably interferes with the liberty of parents and guardians to direct the upbringing and education of children under their control. . . . The fundamental theory of liberty upon which all governments of this Union repose excludes any general power of the State to standardize its children by forcing them to accept instruction from public teachers only. The child is not the mere creature of the State; those who nurture him and direct his destiny have the right, coupled with the high duty, to recognize and prepare him for additional obligations.

Similar statements may be quoted to indicate the position of the Roman Catholic church. For example, in 1946, it was said that the state's "role in education is in reality secondary and supplementary to that of the home," and further that "the concept of the primary rights of parents in education is not only legally basic to the American system of schools, but fundamentally vital to the existence of

---

11. Fogg v. Board of Education, 76 N.H. 296, 82 Atl. 173 (1912).

our democracy." According to this view, "the function of the state in education is, not to monopolize and control the schools, but to protect and assist the parents in the fulfillment of their obligation to provide adequate educational opportunities for their children."[12]

However, it seems to be generally accepted, in statute and decision by legislature and court alike, that the language of Justice McReynolds is not to be considered as stating the predominant theory of child control and education. It is society generally, operating through the state governments, that has primary control—that has the right to prescribe the minimum standards of education the child should have. Education of all the youthful is a matter of vital public concern. The very foundations of the democratic system of government are believed to depend, in substantial measure at least, upon the existence of a literate, knowledgeable citizenry. More than that, the very survival of the United States as a nation is thought to be keyed to the availability of a continuing flow of trained technical specialists from the nation's school systems to places in industry and related areas. Known shortages of trained engineers, for example, is a matter of great concern today. Other areas exist in which the demand for competent manpower exceeds the supply.[13]

Thus it is for two reasons that education is of major public concern and cannot be left to the individual choice

---

12. The statements quoted are taken from McLaughlin, *op. cit. supra* note 5 at 188. See Gardner, "Liberty, The State, and The School," 20 *Law and Contemporary Problems* 184 (1955).

13. Recently a number of pronouncements have been made on the urgent need for more technicians and scientists. See, for example, *New York Times*, May 21, 1956, p. 1; *Life*, March 5, 1956.

of the parents of the child. Whereas, when viewed historically, mass education has been the ideal and the goal, today it has become a necessity. The time is past when the nation can afford a large group of partial or complete illiterates. We have entered a period in which the machine has either replaced or is replacing the untrained human being, both in the manual tasks and in the menial mental tasks. An incredibly rapid technological change has, in the space of a few years, done away with the need for the untrained and unskilled and has scarcely any place for the slightly trained. At the same time, an enormous demand has been created for the technician, for the person of technical ability, for the slide-rule operator who can handle and perhaps even understand the machines he manipulates. All of this means that education has become more than a luxury for the betterment of the individual by providing a means to improve his status; it has become a necessity without which the economy would falter, the national security would be imperiled, and the democratic system repudiated.

So, education there must be—and there will be. The point is important in any scrutiny of the private school system of the United States. It can thus be said with some degree of certainty that, even with the doctrine of the *Pierce* case, the private school will be allowed to remain in operation only so long as it continues to fulfill what society, i.e., the people generally, has set forth as minimum educational requirements and as the type and degree of training considered desirable or necessary. How does this notion fit in with the legal doctrine?

State Control Over Private Education

There seems to be considerable uncertainty in the legal doctrine regarding the extent to which a state may go in controlling the administration of private schools. It may be, however, that this uncertainty is more apparent than real; its basis could well be the relative paucity of court decisions as compared to legislative enactments and the tendency of lawyers trained in the common-law tradition to emphasize the case over the statute in finding authoritative doctrine. As mentioned above, there are few United States Supreme Court decisions directly in point: in addition to the *Pierce* and *Meyer* cases only the *Dartmouth College* case[14] and *Berea College v. Kentucky*[15] are relevant. And both of the latter are, in essence, of minor importance to the present inquiry. In the *Dartmouth College* case the Supreme Court ruled that a charter granted to a private institution is in the nature of a contract and cannot be revoked or altered without the consent of those to whom it was granted. The basis for the decision, which was rendered in 1816, was the part of the Constitution prohibiting state legislation that impairs the obligation of contracts. The force of this decision has been greatly reduced, however, through widespread use of reservations in the charters granted to corporations, including those of private schools. The *Berea College* case involved a Kentucky statute making it unlawful to intermingle white and Negro students in a private school; it will be more fully discussed below. Suffice it for present purposes to say that the Supreme Court reached its de-

14. Trustees of Dartmouth College v. Woodward, 4 Wheat. (U.S.) 518 (1816).
15. 211 U.S. 45 (1908).

cision without finding it necessary to rule on the constitutionality of such a statute.

The litigation that has taken place in state courts does serve to establish, in conjunction with the state legislation, certain fairly clear, albeit still uncertain, lines of doctrine concerning the private school and state authority. Speaking generally, there is no doubt that substantial intervention by state authority is permissible and is widely practiced throughout the nation. This intervention in the affairs of private schools falls into three categories: curriculum, instruction, and administration, with some overlap existing.

Curriculum.—In *Meyer v. Nebraska,* the Supreme Court held that a state may not prohibit the teaching of the German language and other subjects that "cannot reasonably be regarded as harmful." Nevertheless, it is true that English is the required medium of instruction in many states. In addition, certain subjects are frequently required to be taught in all the schools of the state. Examples are the Constitution, history, and American government. In other states, such subjects as physical training, traffic regulation, and the effects upon the human system of alcoholic stimulants, narcotics, and poisonous substances must be given. Some states have extremely detailed curriculum requirements; an example is Pennsylvania, which by statute requires that "in every elementary public and private school, established and maintained in this Commonwealth, the following subjects shall be taught, in the English language and from English texts: English, including spelling, reading, and writing, arithmetic, geography, the history of the United States and of Pennsylvania, civics, including loyalty to the State and National Government, safety education, and the humane treatment of birds and animals, health, including physical training and physiology, music, and art."[16]

As a general proposition, it may be said that a state may prescribe certain minimum curriculum requirements to which private schools must adhere. However, it probably cannot prevent the teaching of other subjects, provided that these other subjects are not subversive in nature or inimical to the public order. So far as the latter is concerned, no doubt exists that a state may prohibit any type of educational activity that threatens its own safety or is otherwise not in consonance with the generalized requirements of the state's police powers. The outward limits of the power of state authority to control private school curricula have never been drawn by the United States Supreme Court. There have, however, been some attempts by state courts to do so. *People v. Stanley*,[17] a Colorado case, is an example. There, the Colorado Supreme Court stated that the right to conduct a private school and the right of parents to have their children taught in such schools are liberties guaranteed by the Fourteenth Amendment, subject, however, to the following qualifications: (a) the state may enact compulsory education laws, (b) certain subjects clearly essential to good citizenship may be required, and (c) teachers and the physical location of the schools must be reputable and the subjects taught must neither be immoral nor inimical to the public welfare.

Instruction.—In addition to the actual subjects taught,

---

16. Pa. Stat. Annotated, title 24, § 15-1511. See, for a collection of such statutes, Note, 4 *Intramural Law Review of New York University* 35 (1948); McLaughlin, *supra* note 5.

17. 81 Colo, 276, 255 Pac. 610 (1927).

a state also exercises a measure of control over those who teach private school pupils. The private school teacher must meet standards of competency established by the state. Statutes in many states require that teachers in private schools must obtain and possess the same certification as public school teachers. In other states, teachers in both private and public schools are required to take an oath to support the state and federal constitutions.[18]

Administration.—The third general type of state control over private schools relates to the administration of the schools. As in the other types, such control follows as a natural concomitant of the fact that a state may compel attendance in a school and that private schools may be substituted by parents for the public schools as the medium through which this societal duty is fulfilled. Control over administration runs from the trivial to the important. For instance, some states have prescribed that fire drills must be carried out periodically, while others have established certain sanitary standards to be met. More importantly, other states provide for supervision and inspection of the private schools, the keeping of certain records, and the rendering of reports to state officials. Length of the school terms have, in like manner, been the subject of regulation.[19]

Appraisal

Although the principle is firmly established that private (including denominational) education is an acceptable substitute for public school education—so much so that it has been given constitutional protection—this has

18. E.g., in Colorado, New York, and South Dakota.
19. McLaughlin, *supra* note 5, collects the relevant statutes.

not been followed to its logical conclusion. It has been met with a countervailing principle that there is an important societal interest in the education of the nation's youth. Accordingly, state control over private education is an established fact, meeting such little disagreement that the state statutes spelling out that control have met few challenges in the courts. Significant areas in the management of the private school, including curriculum and administration, are subject to governmental supervision.

Private schools exist because they predated public schools historically and, more importantly, because they allow for the fulfillment of certain goals not obtainable in the public schools. Chief of these is that of religious training. Constitutionally banned from the public schools, religion and religious training seems to be the principal difference between the two school systems so far as what is offered the pupil is concerned. Other differences exist, but they relate to matters other than offerings of the curriculum. And the differences do not concern matters considered to be fundamental by the people as a whole. Private education does fulfill, at least adequately and often doubtless in a superior fashion, the minimum standards of education established by society. An appraisal of the statutes and judicial decisions leads to the conclusion that, even with the *Pierce* and *Meyer* cases, there is a sufficient societal interest in education to make the continuation of that record necessary for the survival of the private school. In other words, so long as the private school continues to fulfill the minimum educational objectives of society, it will be allowed to continue and to flourish. That it does so now is evident in the minimal character of the control over private education exercised in fact by state governments.

AN EVALUATION

It is evident that private education occupies an important position in the American system of education. Undoubtedly it will continue to do so. Parents will continue to have the choice of sending their children either to a public school or to a school that meets minimum standards but is administered privately. The basic pattern of education, as established and maintained for decades, will not be altered. But whether a private school can escape feeling the impact of the Supreme Court's segregation decision is another question, one as yet unanswered.

What importance does the decision in the *Segregation Cases* have for the private and denominational school administrator? This broad question has several facets: (a) Suppose that it was decided to admit Negroes to a hitherto all-white private school. What governmental sanctions, if any, exist that are intended to prevent such action? Are such sanctions valid under the federal Constitution? What sanctions of a nongovernmental character could an administrator of an integrating private school anticipate? Similarly, are privately-imposed sanctions legally valid? (b) Is there any likelihood that the doctrine enunciated in the *Segregation Cases* can be extended to apply to the admission policies of the nonpublic school? This question raises the further question: Is the conduct of nonpublic education "state action" within the reach of the proscriptions of the Fourteenth Amendment? A subsidiary question is: If a private educational institution is considered to be performing a public function so as to be within the "state action" requirement of the Fourteenth Amendment, does that mean that a parochial school would then violate the establishment of religion clause of the First Amendment? (c) Suppose there is a trust fund set up for the education of whites. May a nonwhite person invoke the judicial process so as to benefit from the trust? Conversely, may the trustee alter the terms of the trust so as to include nonwhite persons among the beneficiaries? This problem involves the broader question of whether recent pronouncements on racial matters by the Supreme Court and the President have established a national policy against racial discrimination. (d) Assuming a grant of property to a private school, with the grantor reserving a right to recover the property should it be used for other than education for whites, would the operation of that clause require judicial action and thus fall within the doctrine of the restrictive covenant cases? In other words, would court enforcement of such a clause be state action within the Fourteenth Amendment and thus prohibited under existing law?

The ensuing chapters will discuss these questions in detail, setting out the legal doctrine with as much precision as the various subject matters allow and forecasting the probable course of future judicial decision. Some of what will be discussed travels judicial seas as yet uncharted, and thus must perforce be cast in language considerably qualified.

CHAPTER TWO

GOVERNMENTAL SANCTIONS AGAINST INTEGRATION

THE PLACE of the private school as an integral part of the American school system has been secure since the decision in 1923 of the United States Supreme Court in the *Pierce* case. However, the limits of the power of state governments to regulate those schools has never been definitively clarified. That the state can regulate is clear; still obscure and ill-defined are the limits of that power. That some restraints do exist is a necessary conclusion from the *Pierce* decision and from the nature of the American system of constitutional government.

By and large, state control has taken the form of measures designed to insure that the private school at least meets the standards to which the public schools ostensibly adhere. The main idea has been for the state to prescribe minimum standards in certain areas deemed of particular importance, e.g., curriculum and faculty, and to allow the private school free rein in other areas. One of the latter areas has been the admission practices of private schools. Whereas all states have detailed legislation and regulations regarding admission to the public schools, most have not seen fit to concern themselves with the private schools. So far as race or religion is concerned, several states have legislated so-called Fair Educational Practices Acts designed to require that certain private schools ignore race or religion as a criterion for matriculation.[1] On the other hand, a number of Southern states have statutes that appear to require racial segregation in nonpublic schools. These statutes range from out-and-out prohibition of racial intermixture to the imposing of criminal sanctions against those who attempt integration of white and colored students. This chapter will outline and discuss these statutes.

Of course, racial separation, even in those states where it has not been required, has been a fact of life in private education. Only a few schools, mostly universities, have not had racial restrictions as part of their admission policies. Even in those schools where Negroes have been allowed to enter—Yale and Harvard come to mind—they have been but a handful. Even today, the "white" private school that has accepted large numbers of Negro students does not exist.[2]

Our discussion of the attempts by state legislatures to prescribe admission standards for private schools can

---

[1] A good discussion of these statutes may be found in Note, 64 *Harvard Law Review* 307 (1950).

[2] The principle of racial integration of course does not depend upon the numbers of students formerly excluded who are now admitted. But it should be pointed out that the problems involved in desegregation are virtually nonexistent when only a handful of Negroes are admitted as compared to the problems that would arise if, say, fifty percent of the student body were colored. For example, Yale's problems several years ago when Levi Jackson, a Negro, matriculated and later became captain of the football team are hardly to be equated with the problems now facing Archbishop Rummel in the Roman Catholic parochial schools in Louisiana.

See the following articles for discussions of racial integration in the North and South: Johnson, "Racial Integration in Public Higher Education in the South," 23 *Journal of Negro Education* 317 (1954); Johnson, "Racial Integration in Southern Higher Education," 34 *Social Forces* 309 (1956); Plaut, "Racial Integration in Higher Education in the North," 23 *Journal of Negro Education* 310 (1954).

begin with a case decided in 1908 by the United States Supreme Court. The case is *Berea College v. Kentucky*.[3] A Kentucky statute made it "unlawful for any person, corporation or association of persons to maintain or operate any college, school or institution where persons of the white and negro races are both received as pupils for instruction. . . ." Berea College, a coeducational, nondenominational institution, was established in 1855. Beginning in 1866 it began to admit Negroes, treating them exactly as it did its white students. The Kentucky legislation came in 1904, was violated by Berea's administration, upheld by the state's highest court, and ultimately challenged in the United States Supreme Court as a deprivation of liberty and property protected by the due process clause of the Fourteenth Amendment to the Constitution. That amendment reads in pertinent part as follows: "No State shall . . . deprive any person of life, liberty, or property, without due process of law. . . ."

The Court thus had a direct opportunity to rule on the constitutional validity of state prescription of admission standards of private schools. It chose, however, to reject that opportunity and upheld the legislation, pinning its decision not on constitutional grounds but on the power a state has over a corporation to amend its charter. The statute was considered to be an amendment to the corporate charter of Berea College. In so ruling the Court gave strong support to the notion that a state can prohibit corporations from giving instruction to a racially mixed student body. To this, Justice Harlan vigorously dissented, stating that he thought the Court "should directly meet

3. 211 U.S. 45 (1908).

and decide the broad [constitutional] question presented by the statute." He then went on to say that the Court should adjudge whether it could be made a crime "to maintain and operate a private institution of learning where white and black pupils are received, at the same time, for instruction." The Justice left no doubt as to what his view would be on that question: "I am of the opinion," he said, "that . . . the statute is an arbitrary invasion of the rights of liberty and property guaranteed by the Fourteenth Amendment against hostile state action and is, therefore, void." He did not prevail, however, and since that time the United States Supreme Court has not had to face the question.

The rather unique circumstances involved in the *Berea College* case make it one that is of interest but not of controlling authority over possible present-day cases.[4] It did, of course, uphold indirectly the power of a state to require separation of the races in private schools. But the constitutional question was not met by the majority of the Supreme Court. Since there have been no other cases since the decision in the *Berea College* case, that question is still an unsettled one. It will be discussed in some detail in the latter part of this chapter.

STATE STATUTES APPEARING TO REQUIRE RACIAL
SEGREGATION IN PRIVATE SCHOOLS

Since the Supreme Court decision in the *Segregation Cases* in May, 1954, governmental officials in most of the Southern states have made strenuous attempts to avoid the

---

4. The changes in racial relations that have taken place in the last half-century could well make the *Berea College* case a historical curiosity. It is of interest to note, also, that Berea is again an integrated institution.

impact of those decisions in the various state public school systems. Doctrines of "interposition," long dormant, have been resurrected and dusted off in six states; through these efforts it is hoped that the racial separateness of the public schools will be continued indefinitely.[5] Other actions of the Southern state officials have been to institute a statutory basis for a system of "private schools," to be established at such time as a court orders the entry of a Negro student into some public school formerly limited to whites only.[6] Neither of these actions concerns our present inquiry. However, in at least two states—Mississippi and Louisiana —the legislatures in 1956 considered bills that would seek to prevent (or punish) desegregation of nonpublic schools.

After Archbishop Rummel of the Roman Catholic church announced that the parochial schools of Louisiana would be racially integrated, an immediate furor broke out. In addition to strong protests from many Catholic laymen in Louisiana, bills were introduced into the legislature to take away the tax benefits of any denominational or private school that integrated and to deny any state benefits to such schools. The bills, however, failed of enactment.[7] Similarly, in Mississippi the legislature failed to enact com-

    5. The interposition movement in the South is exhaustively discussed in a series of articles entitled "The Doctrine of Interposition: A Round Table," 5 *Journal of Public Law* 1 (1956). See also Miller, "The Interposition Gambit," 11 *New South* No. 6, p. 4 (June, 1956); and the unsigned article, "Interposition vs. Judicial Power," 1 *Race Relations Law Reporter* 465 (1956).
    6. These actions are discussed in McKay, "'With All Deliberate Speed': A Study of School Desegregation," 31 *New York University Law Review* 991 (1956).
    7. *Southern School News*, July, 1956, lists the Louisiana legislative actions taken to preserve segregation.

parable proposals for invoking sanctions against a desegregating private school.

These actions, although abortive, indicate the type of adversity that can befall the private school in some Southern states. Other than direct prohibition of interracial private education, such as the action that took place in Kentucky and led to the *Berea College* decision, actions by state authorities seeking to prevent integration of private schools fall into two broad categories. On the one hand, some state statutes purport to deny benefits otherwise obtainable, while on the other, some statutes seek to impose personal punishment upon those involved—the students, the teachers who instruct them, and the administrators who admit them. While relatively rare at the present time, provisions for these stiff sanctions do exist. Accordingly, they merit detailed attention.

Denial of Benefits

Control over education and educational matters is one of the powers reserved for the states in accordance with the Tenth Amendment to the Constitution. Therefore, in the absence of a provision to the contrary in its constitution there is nothing to prevent a state from conferring benefits upon privately controlled educational institutions. While it may be, as we will note below, that the equal protection clause of the Fourteenth Amendment to the federal Constitution requires that a benefit accorded one private school must be tendered similarly to all, there has been no litigation on the point. The only provision of the federal Constitution to have been brought into play with regard to benefits for private schools is the "establishment of religion" clause of the First Amendment. Some litigation has arisen in recent years about sectarian education—schools controlled or operated by religious groups—resulting in the enunciation of the so-called "wall of separation" doctrine. Under this doctrine, it is held that a state is forbidden by the First Amendment either to allow the use of public school buildings for the furtherance of religion or to support religion or religious institutions, including those devoted to education.[8]

However, the no-establishment-of-religion doctrine has not prevented the Supreme Court from upholding the constitutionality of state legislation that confers certain benefits upon denominational as well as other private schools. One of the most important of these benefits is that of exemption from taxation of private school property. All states have such a practice and it has never been seriously challenged.[9] In like fashion, some states have made provision for the distribution of textbooks free of charge to pupils of private schools as well as to those attending public schools. This the Supreme Court found to be a valid practice.[10] And some states have established a system of free bus transportation for such students; again, this has been found to be within the Constitution.[11]

8. Among the many discussions of the relationship of church and state in the United States, see Pfeffer, *Church, State and Freedom* (1953); O'Neill, *Religion and Education Under the Constitution* (1949).
9. See the discussions in Elliott and Chambers, *The Colleges and the Courts* 285-350 (1936); McLaughlin, *A History of State Legislation Affecting Private Elementary and Secondary Schools in the United States, 1870-1945* (1946); Note, 3 *Intramural Law Review of New York University* 147 (1948).
10. Cochran v. Board of Education, 281 U.S. 370 (1930).
11. Everson v. Board of Education, 330 U.S. 1 (1947). Both the *Everson* case and the *Cochran* case, *supra* note 10, are bottomed on the theory that the state is aiding and benefiting the pupil, not the religious school, in giving free textbooks and bus transportation; the Supreme Court is careful to point out that "a wall of separation" exists and must be

No serious disagreement exists on the question of tax exemptions for the private schools. On the other subsidies, however, major controversy has arisen. Despite the fact that the Supreme Court has indicated that there is no objection under the federal Constitution to giving books and other aid, a number of state constitutions expressly forbid any subvention to sectarian schools other than tax exemptions. Speaking parenthetically, this is an interesting differentiation: tax exemptions, dollar-wise at least, are much more important than, say, bus transportation or even textbooks; yet it is on the monetarily unimportant benefits that controversy arises. The most important subsidy meets no opposition.

Benefits of these types are readily available for use by a state administration wishing to prevent a private school from removing racial restrictions on admission. The idea is simple: What the state gives, the state can take away. Subsidies should not be given to those who do not support the basic policies of the state; benefits should be denied those who are considered to be undermining "the way of life" of the particular state. Diversity, in other words, is a sin, conformity to imposed norms a virtue—at least so far as racial segregation is concerned. And coercion should be visited upon those who do not conform, upon those who refuse to accept governmental standards of virtue, and upon those who believe that a person who lives in the United States has a right to choose those with whom he would associate.

One state that already has made provision for the

---

maintained between church and state. But of course aid to a pupil of a denominational school cannot avoid being aid to the school and thus an aid to religion.

denial of tax exemptions for an integrating school is Georgia. Long before the current crisis in racial relations developed, Georgia's constitution contained the following provision:

The General Assembly may, by law, exempt from taxation all public property; places of religious worship and burial; all institutions of purely public charity; all intangible personal property owned by or irrevocably held in trust for the exclusive benefit of, religious, educational and charitable institutions, no part of the net profit from the operation of which can inure to the benefit of any private person; all buildings erected for and used as a college, incorporated academy or other seminary of learning, and also all funds or property held or used as endowment by such colleges, incorporated academies or seminaries of learning, provided the same is not invested in real estate; and provided, further, that said exemptions shall only apply to such colleges, incorporated academies or other seminaries of learning as are open to the general public; *provided further, that all endowments to institutions established for white people shall be limited to white people, and all endowments to institutions established for colored people shall be limited to colored people;* . . .[12]

The Georgia legislature has implemented this with a statute that is now part of the Georgia Code. Identical language to that quoted above has been used, including the provision that "all endowments to institutions established for white people, shall be limited to white people, and all endowments to institutions established for colored people, shall be limited to colored people. . . ."[13] The two provisions, constitutional and statutory, operate together in such a fashion that any private school accepting both white and colored students loses its tax exemption. Of

12. Georgia Constitution, Art. VII, § 1, Par. IV, set out in Ga. Code Annotated § 2-5404. Italics supplied by the author.
13. Georgia Code Annotated § 92-201.

course law enforcement officials may choose not to invoke the statutory penalty, particularly if the school that integrates the races does so without fanfare and without publicity. As we will mention subsequently, this has happened in at least one instance.

Georgia's statute has not been tested in court on constitutional grounds. However, it can be readily seen that such legislation immediately raises serious questions as to its validity under the Constitution. There are at least two fundamental objections: Would denial of tax benefits solely on the basis of racial admission policies be a denial of equal protection of the laws as required by the Fourteenth Amendment? If the action is taken against a denominational school, would it be an interference with the practice of religion and thus violative of the "free exercise of religion" clause of the First Amendment? These questions will be discussed in detail below. Suffice it for the moment to say that even if such a statute were eventually declared unconstitutional, the interim difficulties would be considerable; it would take a brave administrator to undertake an attack on the statute or to go ahead without regard to consequences. Severe deprivations could be the result, for the tax exemption amounts to a considerable subsidy—so much so that it could be of crucial importance to the financial viability of the organization.

So far as statutes presently on the books are concerned, the removal of tax exemptions is apparently the only type of direct sanction available that would involve the denial of a state-granted benefit. However, other subventions in favor of nonpublic education exist, and it would be possible for a state administration to get enabling legislation through what normally is an acquiescent legislature.[14] Benefits so affected include free school books and writing materials, hot lunches, and similar grants that, when challenged, have been interpreted as grants to the individual students rather than to the schools. In like fashion, free bus transportation could be taken away.

Again, whether these actions would hold up under attack on constitutional grounds would depend upon the manner in which the statutes are drawn and the manner in which they are administered. An argument, developed below, could be made on equal protection grounds that singling out integrating schools for such action would be an unreasonable classification and thus proscribed by the Fourteenth Amendment. And if the statute purported to treat all private schools, whether integrating or not, alike, it could still be open to attack constitutionally if in fact it was being administered in an uneven way.

Another possible sanction under this category does not as yet exist on the statute books, but it would seem to be at least theoretically possible. This is the accreditation of graduates of private schools seeking admission in the public school system (e.g., the accreditation of graduates of private preparatory schools enrolling in the state university) could be keyed to the admission practices of the private school. In other words, it appears possible that a state could, if it chose, deny graduates of integrated private schools the opportunity to attend a public school. This could be done by statute or, with an appropriate delegation

14. The fact that legislation was introduced in the 1956 sessions of the Mississippi and Louisiana legislatures to deny benefits to integrating private schools, but that this legislation failed of enactment, should not be considered to be conclusive. The fact of such integration had yet to take place.

of authority, by administrative regulation. Whether valid or not, the argument could be made that graduates of integrated schools are ill-equipped to utilize the benefits of a higher education.[15] Such a sanction would, of course, operate against the students themselves and only indirectly against the school. To the extent placed in practice, however, it would tend to exercise an influence over the actions of the administration of a private school. Similar constitutional objections to those noted above would, however, be available.

Criminal Punishment

The broad group of powers usually called the police power provides the basis for the other general type of sanction that could be invoked against a private school. The police power can only be loosely defined: it means that a state has power to protect the health, safety, and morals of its population and may legislate for the general welfare. Other than those appearing in state constitutions, its only limitations are those of the federal Constitution, chiefly the due process and equal protection clauses of the Fourteenth Amendment plus those parts of the first eight

---

15. See McLaughlin, *supra* note 9, at 80: "A possibility of considerable indirect control [of private schools by the state] was implicit in a regulation which required pupils coming from nonpublic schools to take an examination in order to determine their proper assignment to grades in the public school system. A school board in Parsons, Kansas, passed a rule that pupils from a private or parochial school would be required to pass an entrance examination in order to enter the high school. The regulation was opposed as an arbitrary and unreasonable discrimination between private school and public school pupils, and as a violation of the constitutional right of all children to attend the public schools. The court ruled, however, that the requirement of an examination of students from private schools was reasonable as a means of determining the proper placement of pupils and a matter wholly within the discrimination of the board."

amendments that have been judicially read into the Fourteenth Amendment.

The police power may be used in two ways by a state administration bent on punishing a private school: statutes could be passed imposing criminal punishment, by fine or imprisonment or both, upon those concerned; and the general statutes aimed at protecting the public order could be used in a stringent fashion by law enforcement officials who wished to harass the school and those in charge of it. Some existing laws on the statute books of Kentucky, Tennessee, and Oklahoma illustrate the first type; the actions taken by law enforcement officials of Alabama and Louisiana against the National Association for the Advancement of Colored People indicate what can be done under the second.

Tennessee's statutes may be quoted to indicate the precise nature of the criminal sanctions that could be invoked. Three sections of the Tennessee Code are relevant:

49-3701. Interracial schools prohibited.—It shall be unlawful for any school, academy, college, or other place of learning to allow white and colored persons to attend the same school, academy, college, or other place of learning.

49-3702. Teaching of mixed classes prohibited.—It shall be unlawful for any teacher, professor, or educator in any college, academy, or school of learning, to allow the white and colored races to attend the same school, or for any teacher or educator, or other person to instruct or teach both the white and colored races in the same class, school, or college building, or in any other place or places of learning, or allow or permit the same to be done with their knowledge, consent, or procurement.

49-3703. Penalty for violations.—Any person violating any of the provisions of this chapter, shall be guilty of a misdemeanor, and, upon conviction, shall be fined for each offense fifty dollars

($50.00), and imprisonment not less than thirty (30) days nor more than six (6) months.[16]

Oklahoma has similar statutes, but go a step further: provision is there made for fines and punishment "for any white person [attending] any school, college, or institution where colored persons are received as pupils for instruction."[17] Florida and Kentucky seek to prohibit interracial private education but do not provide for any punishment for violations. Florida's statute contains the flat prohibition: "No individual, body of individuals, corporation or association shall conduct within this state any school of any grade (public, private or parochial) wherein white persons and negroes are instructed or boarded in the same building or taught in the same classes or at the same time by the same teachers."[18] Kentucky prohibits operation of integrated schools as well as an instructor teaching in or a student attending any "college, school or institution" where persons of both the white and colored races are received as pupils or receive instruction.[19]

The basic theory of American government and American jurisprudence—that the government is one of "laws, not of men" operating under the general supervision of "The Rule of Law"—presupposes that the law will be administered evenly, objectively, and without preference or prejudice. Justice is blindfolded and operates, so the theory goes, without the need for determinative intervention by fallible human beings.[20] It has, of course, long

---

16. Tennessee Code Annotated (1955).
17. Oklahoma Statutes, Title 70, § 5-7 (1951).
18. Florida Statutes Annotated § 228.09 (1943).
19. Kentucky Revised Statutes § 158.020 (1953).
20. This is one of the fundamental concepts of traditional democratic theory. It is perhaps not facetious to point out that Judge Jerome Frank

been recognized that not only is this an ideal and not a reality, but more than that, it is an ideal that is impossible of attainment. Law is not self-executing; it requires the thought processes of human beings before it can operate. This fact, which should be obvious but which nevertheless is all too seldom recognized, sets the stage for the second type of police-power action that could be taken against a private school integrating the races.

The vast discretion exercised by law enforcement officials, even though subject to being checked by the courts should excesses occur, gives those officials an enormous power of harassment. Given sufficient incentive, they can bring tremendous pressure to bear upon individuals unfortunate enough to incur their displeasure. None of this type of action will be illegal; all of it will, ostensibly at least, be aimed at enforcement of the law. But nevertheless, the real intention will be to cause annoyance or embarrassment or harassment to the object of the official action.

A possible example of this type of subtle punitive action is that recently taken against the NAACP in Louisiana and Alabama. In March, 1956, Louisiana officials brought an action to enjoin the NAACP from continuing operations in that state until the organization had filed with the Louisiana Secretary of State the names and addresses of all its members and officers. The injunction has been granted, and the NAACP has ceased operations in Louisiana pend-

---

once remarked that a government of laws and not of men inevitably resulted in "a government of lawyers, not of men." A recent restatement of the concept may be found in Freund, "The Rule of Law," [1956] *Washington University Law Quarterly* 314.

ing appeal.[21] The injunction was granted pursuant to a statute originally enacted in 1924 as an anti-Ku Klux Klan measure.

The highly publicized bus boycott in Montgomery, Alabama, by Negroes in an effort to end bus segregation led finally to the indictment of the boycott leaders under an old city ordinance originally enacted for use in labor disputes. Then in June, 1956, the NAACP was enjoined from further activity in Alabama after the state Attorney General had brought an action alleging that the NAACP's actions "have resulted in violation of our laws and tend in many instances to create a breach of the peace." The chief allegations were that the Negro organization had fostered and led the bus boycott in Montgomery, had "employed or otherwise" paid Miss Autherine Lucy to break down segregation barriers at the University of Alabama, and

21. See McKay, *supra* note 6, at 1059-60 for a brief discussion, in addition to the *Southern School News* for April, May, June, and July, 1956. An example of this type of activity taken from a Northern city and having nothing to do with racial relations appeared in *Newsweek* for July 23, 1956, pp. 46-47: "The Federal agents who moved in on Reading, Pa., on July 5, to the complete surprise, perhaps even the astonishment, of the city's mayor and police force, were acting on tips from *The Times* and *The Eagle*, the jointly owned local dailies. The raiders seized 44 pinball and slot machines in 23 taverns and hotels, including a bar once owned by the mayor . . . and now operated by his brother. For their enterprise on behalf of the law, the two Reading newspapers were rewarded last week with systematic bullying by both mayor and police. The next Monday, July 9, reporters were locked out of the press room at City Hall on the mayor's claim that the space was needed for other purposes. . . . [The political reporter for *The Times*] was arrested [on the steps of City Hall] on charges of 'creating a nuisance' and 'holding up traffic'; the court gave him his choice of a $51.25 fine or 30 days in jail. . . . More aggravating was police treatment of the newspapers' delivery trucks. Cop cars trailed them on their rounds and handed them 73 tickets for double parking, blocking crosswalks, and stopping in bus zones. . . . Mayor McDevitt admitted ordering the war on Reading's dailies but defended his action against 'press lords' and 'smart-aleck' reporters: 'I merely used the weapons I could in the public interest.' "

had "never qualified to do business in Alabama as a foreign corporation."[22]

The same techniques are available for use by state officials against private school administrators who mix the races. Given the desire on the part of an attorney general or district attorney, a complaisant judge would probably not be too difficult to find. While ultimately such actions would probably be invalidated on constitutional grounds, that would take a long time; in the interim, a great deal of annoyance or worse would be suffered. The ideal of blindfolded justice can be, and often is, shattered by the operational reality of a prejudicial thumb on the scales.

THE CONSTITUTIONAL BASIS OF GOVERNMENTAL SANCTIONS

It may well be that state law enforcement officials will choose to ignore violations of law and thus the sanctions discussed above may never be invoked. Should an individual private school quietly decide to admit Negro students and do so without publicity, quite possibly nothing would be done about it. This has in fact happened in

22. See *Southern School News*, July, 1956, p. 10. Compare the following action taken in Americus, Georgia: "Superior Court Judge Cleveland Rees Monday at Americus postponed until July 19 a hearing on an injunction to ban permanently the operation of a summer camp which operated last summer on a nonsegregated basis. The Sumter County commissioners obtained on June 8 a temporary injunction which prevented opening of the camp on June 18 and now seek to make the ban permanent on health grounds. Monday's postponement was granted at the request of [the] county attorney.... The County's petition does not mention race but bases its argument on an alleged lack of proper sanitary and health facilities at the campsite.... Four Sumter County farmers ... have sought to associate themselves with the county in the injunction action, claiming in their petition the sponsors have no license and would operate the camp 'in a manner detrimental to morals.' They claimed specifically young children at the camp would be allowed to see pigs being born. The camp is a religious communal enterprise in which about 60 whites and Negroes are associated." The Atlanta *Constitution*, July 3, 1956.

some isolated instances in the South: some private schools have admitted Negroes for a number of years and this, although certainly known to state officials, has received no adverse reaction.[23] The reason appears to be simple: Since the admissions are not publicized and are not widely known, the officials are not called upon to take a public position or to make a decision in the matter. Their hand has not been forced. If it were otherwise, the result could only be that the officials would enforce the punitive statutes.

The governmental sanctions, whether a denial of state benefit or punitive action, would if enforced undoubtedly be attacked on federal constitutional grounds. The relevant provisions that could be invoked are those that have the effect of precluding arbitrary action on the part of state governments: the due process and equal protection clauses of the Fourteenth Amendment ("No State shall ... deprive any person of life, liberty, or property, without due process of law; nor deny to any person within its jurisdiction the equal protection of the laws"); and, for denominational schools, the religious freedom clause in the First Amendment ("Congress shall make no law ... prohibiting the free exercise [of religion]"), which has been made a limitation also on state governments through judicial interpretation.

In the absence of a precise, fully developed factual situation out of which such a constitutional problem has arisen, it is difficult to foresee all of the possible variations the problem might take. Additionally, it is difficult to

---

23. A list of integrating private schools has been compiled by the Southern Regional Council, Inc., 63 Auburn Ave., N.E., Atlanta, Georgia, and is available in mimeographed form.

forecast the manner in which the Supreme Court would approach any given case; it has a variety of techniques available, of which one or a combination of several would be chosen depending upon the peculiar factual situation involved. Even so, arguments on Fourteenth Amendment grounds would proceed substantially as follows. Suppose that a private school integrated the races; suppose further that a state administration enforced a statute requiring the denial of tax exemptions for such schools, but did not remove tax exemptions generally or for other private schools. Whether that would amount to a denial of the standards of equality of treatment required by the equal protection clause would depend upon the answer given to the further question of whether the state had made an "unreasonable classification." For the Supreme Court has stated many times that the Constitution does not forbid a state's making some classifications, but only those which are unreasonable or arbitrary and without a rational basis. The answer to that question is not self-evident; there is no direct authority in point.

Nevertheless, it would appear likely that action taken only against a school that integrates the races, with no concomitant action taken to remove all tax exemptions from all schools, would fall under an attack on equal protection grounds. While the Fourteenth Amendment is not a doctrinaire requirement of the impractical—reasonable distinctions and classifications are permitted—it does forbid invidious discrimination; it requires laws of like application to all who are similarly situated. Thus the result in the *Segregation Cases:* a classification based solely on race is "unreasonable" and arbitrary and, accordingly, improper under the equal protection clause. Would the same type of reasoning carry over and be applied in the event of denial of tax exemptions because of racial integration? It is likely that it would.

The cases are relatively rare, but it seems clear that the same concepts apply whether the state action in question seeks to impose deprivations (e.g., taxation or school segregation) or to extend benefits (e.g., tax exemptions or free textbooks). A tax exemption to one school or church would have to be extended to other schools and churches falling into the same category. And the converse would appear to be valid: denial of a benefit accorded to all in a category, the benefit being denied because of admission practices contrary to public fiat, would be an "unreasonable" classification. The reason for this is that the state, under constitutional proscription against distinctions based on race, could scarcely be allowed to use race as a means of classification in extending or denying benefits. Racial discriminations, in other words, when made by an organ of the state government, are unreasonable and arbitrary and cannot be used in an effort to control individual behavior. This would seem to be true even though, as Corwin has pointed out, a state's "latitude of discretion is notably wide in the classification of property for purposes of taxation and the granting of partial or total exemption on the grounds of policy...."[24]

The result would be the same should the state, by statute, eliminate all exemptions from taxation for all private schools, but through administration of assessments for taxation impose in fact an unequal burden upon those

---

24. Corwin (editor), *Constitution of the United States of America Annotated* 1152 (1953).

schools integrating the races.[25] In such an event, the school aggrieved by such discrimination in fact would be entitled to have its assessment reduced to the level of others similarly situated;[26] for the equal protection clause not only prohibits "discriminating and partial legislation ... in favor of particular persons as against others in like condition,"[27] it also applies to the manner in which law is administered. "Though the law itself be fair on its face and impartial in appearance, yet, if it is applied and administered by public authority with an evil eye and an unequal hand, so as practically to make unjust and illegal discriminations between persons in similar circumstances, material to their rights, the denial of equal justice is still within the prohibition of the Constitution."[28] More than a mere error would have to be shown, however, to be able to invoke the constitutional guarantee; it would take a purposive, deliberate discrimination.[29]

Governmental sanctions for interracial private education through denial of state-granted benefits would, then, probably be found unconstitutional. If the action were to be taken only against the transgressing school, it would seem to be a clear case; and the same applies if all benefits are removed but the administration of, say, taxation is in fact unequal.

Turning now to the other type of official sanction that might be visited upon a private school administrator, teacher, or student—action under the police power—

---
25. Compare Sunday Lake Iron Co. v. Wakefield, 247 U.S. 350 (1918) with Coulter v. Louisville & Nashville Ry., 196 U.S. 599 (1905).
26. Sioux City Bridge Co. v. Dakota County, 260 U.S. 441, 446 (1923).
27. Minneapolis & St. Louis Ry. v. Beckwith, 129 U.S. 26, 29 (1889).
28. Yick Wo v. Hopkins, 118 U.S. 356, 373 (1886).
29. See Snowden v. Hughes, 321 U.S. 1, 8 (1944).

another constitutional question is posed. The problem is whether the state's action accords with the constitutional concept of due process of law. And it is "substantive" due process, as distinguished from the "procedural" variety, that is the focus of our interest. The problem is one of the substance of the state action or state legislation, not of the manner in which it is administered; that is to say, we assume a regularity of procedure and look instead to what is being done. And again, the two-pronged manner in which the police power of a state may be used will result in a separate discussion for each aspect.

There are no cases directly on the point of whether a state may constitutionally impose criminal penalties for biracial private education, unless the *Berea College* case is considered to be one.[30] Since the question is essentially one of whether a state may impose admission standards on private schools, the result would probably hinge upon the extent to which the Supreme Court would be willing to extend the doctrine of the *Pierce* and *Meyer* cases (discussed in Chapter One). In those cases, the Court held that a state may not, consistent with due process, prohibit private education in toto or prevent the teaching of the German language in a private school. Or, to put it another way, the result could depend upon the extent to which the Court would extend the principle of the *Segregation Cases* to private education. In either event, the problem for the Court would be to determine whether the legislation imposing criminal penalties, and thus effectively preventing biracial private education, had a rational basis or whether it was purely arbitrary. The validity of state exercises of

---

30. Justice Harlan, dissenting in the *Berea College* case, did not believe that the Court had ruled on the constitutional issue.

the police power rests upon whether the means employed by the state (i.e., the statute) bears a real and substantial relation to an end that is public—that is, the public health, safety, or morals, or some other phase of the general welfare.[31]

The end sought by the state thus must be legitimate, and the means utilized to reach that end must be neither arbitrary nor oppressive. Despite the recent swing to broad concepts of substantive due process under which states may freely experiment in economic and social affairs, there has been a concurrent tendency for the Supreme Court to construe state limitations on personal liberties strictly. The normal presumption of constitutionality of state legislative action is, so some believe, reversed in personal liberties cases, with the result that there is a presumption of invalidity of anything that restricts the liberty of the individual.[32] A private school and its administration, faculty, and student body would seem to be one of the liberties protected against arbitrary interference by the due process clause. Some language by the Supreme Court in the *Meyer* and *Pierce* cases is apposite. In *Meyer*, it was said that:

> While . . . [the] Court has not attempted to define with exact-

31. If a police power regulation goes too far, it becomes a taking of liberty or property that the Constitution proscribes. What is "too far," i.e., what is "arbitrary," is of course not susceptible of precise definition but depends upon the rendering of a judgment on the facts and circumstances of each case. See Corwin, *supra* note 24, at 982 *et seq.* for a collection of cases.

32. There is considerable debate on this, both between members of the Supreme Court and also among the commentators, so much so that it is doubtful that more than a few of the individual justices have ever adhered to the notion of the "preferred position" of the First Amendment freedoms. Cf. Jackson, *The Supreme Court in the American System of Government* (1955).

ness the liberty thus guaranteed, the term has received much consideration and some of the included things have been definitely stated. Without doubt, it denotes not merely freedom from bodily restraint but also right of the individual to contract, to engage in any of the common occupations of life, to acquire useful knowledge, . . . and generally to enjoy those privileges long recognized at common law as essential to the orderly pursuit of happiness by free men.[33]

The *Meyer* case is, in substance, an affirmation of the constitutional liberty of a teacher to pursue a lawful calling free and clear of arbitrary restraints imposed by the state.

In the *Pierce* case, the Court said that the "state legislature is not the final judge of limitations of the police power, but its enactment will be set aside when found to be an unwarranted, arbitrary interference with the constitutional right to carry on a lawful business or occupation, and to use and enjoy property," and that the statute requiring compulsory public education "unreasonably interferes with the liberty of parents and guardians to direct the upbringing and education of children under their control."[34] The Court then went on to hold that the corporations involved (i.e., the private schools) were being deprived of their "property" without due process of law.

Now, as we have seen in Chapter One, the state does have constitutional power to regulate in a reasonable manner the activities of private schools. However, it is doubtful that it can, consistent with due process, impose admission standards of racial separation, even though the converse is not true: the state apparently can impose standards of no racial discrimination upon private schools.[35] Requiring

33. 262 U.S. 390, 399 (1923).
34. 268 U.S. 510, 534 (1925).
35. See Note, 64 *Harvard Law Review* 307 (1950).

racial separation anywhere, as distinguished from condoning voluntary segregation by private action, is scarcely permissible and hardly a legitimate use of the state's police powers.[36] It would be an arbitrary action on the part of the state, one proscribed by the due process clause of the Fourteenth Amendment. As was said by federal Judge J. Skelly Wright in a recent case in New Orleans involving use of the police power of Louisiana to compel racial segregation in public schools:

> The problem of changing a people's mores, particularly those with an emotional overlay, is not to be taken lightly. It is a problem which will require the utmost patience, understanding, generosity and forebearance from all of us, of whatever race. But the magnitude of the problem may not nullify the principle. And that principle is that we are, all of us, freeborn Americans, unfettered by sanctions imposed by man because of the work of God.[37]

Not so clear in probable result is the validity under the Constitution of actions taken against an integrating private school based upon general statutes for protection of the public order. On the one hand, action taken by law enforcement officials to insure the most meticulous adherence to the exact letter of all statutes by private school personnel would undoubtedly be entirely valid; at least it would be impossible to prove an improper motive. The regulations relative to sanitation and fire protection are an example of such statutes. While ostensibly only carrying out the law or regulation, state officials conceivably could so harass a private school as to cause a great deal of an-

---

36. See Bush v. Orleans Parish School Board, 138 F. Supp. 337 (E.D.La., 1956) (holding unconstitutional Louisiana's statute requiring racial segregation in public schools on the basis of the police powers).
37. *Ibid.*, at 342.

noyance and expense. Suppose, on the other hand, an action is brought by a state's attorney in which an injunction is sought against a private school for conspiring to violate the state law against racial intermixture. This would probably, as explained above, be invalidated.

The point is that law enforcement officials do have the power, if not the right, to pursue policies and to take action that would result in disturbance and otherwise molest private school personnel. The abstract constitutional principle of protection may be clear enough, but difficulties of proof and the probability of protracted litigation may go far to nullify that protection.[38]

Should the private school concerned be owned or controlled by a religious group, another constitutional argument could be advanced in an attack of official sanctions against an integrating school—the freedom of religion provision of the First Amendment. Since 1940, the limitation against laws prohibiting the free exercise of religion has operated on the states as well as on the national government.[39]

Here, again, no direct authority is available. The states have been singularly loath to attempt any systematic regulation of religion, religious groups, or denominational schools. Some of the language used by Justice Black in his opinion for the Court in *Everson v. Board of Education*,[40] though made in passing, tends to indicate that he at

---

38. A discussion of how police actions at times fail to coincide with constitutional guarantees may be found in Ernst, "The Policeman and Due Process," 2 *Journal of Public Law* 250 (1953). See, also, the example of police action discussed in notes 21 and 22 *supra*.

39. The case so holding was Cantwell v. Connecticut, 310 U.S. 296 (1940).

40. 330 U.S. 1 (1947). In Wood, *Due Process of Law* 85 (1951), the following statement is made: "In the Everson case Justice Black appeared

least believes that a state possibly may have no power to interfere in the conduct of affairs in parochial schools. The *Everson* decision sustained the right of New Jersey to provide free bus transportation to parochial school children. Justice Black's statement, relevant here, was: "[The First Amendment] requires the state to be a neutral in its relations with groups of religious believers and nonbelievers; it does not require the state to be their adversary. State power is no more to be used so as to handicap religions than it is to favor them."

On the other hand, it is clear that while laws "cannot interfere with mere religious belief and opinions, they may with practices."[41] Thus, if the First Amendment is construed so as to permit a man to excuse his conduct on the ground that it involves a religious belief, it would be tantamount to making "the professed doctrines of religious belief superior to the law of the land, and in effect to permit every citizen to become a law unto himself."[42] In other words, as the Court stated in *Cantwell v. Connecticut*, "the [First] Amendment embraces two concepts—freedom to believe and freedom to act. The first is absolute, but in the nature of things, the second cannot be."[43]

The Court has pursued what is at best a rather erratic course in its interpretation of what acts or practices of religion are within the protection of the First Amendment. It is difficult and perhaps even impossible to forecast what

---

to add the idea that to deny the parochial school children the benefits of free transportation would have infringed upon their right to free exercise of their religion."

41. Reynolds v. United States, 98 U.S. 145, 166 (1879).
42. *Ibid.*, at 167.
43. 310 U.S. 296, 303 (1940).

the Court would do with a freedom-of-religion argument aimed at invalidating the official sanctions discussed above. However, if the strong preference in the Constitution for an absence of restraint on religion is added to the fact that the sanctions that could be imposed have little or nothing to do with education—in itself, a legitimate object of governmental concern—the result would seem to be that the use of the sanction would be proscribed. At the very least, the First Amendment point would serve to buttress a decision based on a due process argument.

AN EVALUATION

A discussion has been made of the statutes of some Southeastern states under which sanctions could be imposed upon those connected with a private school attended by both white and colored pupils. These sanctions either deny a state-granted benefit to such a school or provide for criminal penalties. It is fair to say that it is seriously doubtful that such sanctions are constitutional. Should they receive a judicial test, it can be forecast with some confidence that the Supreme Court would adhere to the spirit of the recent racial cases and would strike down attempts to compel private groups to maintain policies of racial separation.

Even so, a private school administration may be reluctant to run the risk of a possible decision upholding the statutes, or to suffer the undoubted difficulties that would ensue in the interim period between the time Negro students were first admitted and final Court decision. It would be possible that the litigation would not reach final resolution for several years. And it is always possible, as noted above, for law enforcement officials to use existing, apparently general, statutes in a manner that would seriously molest the school. There would be, in addition, a number of nongovernmental sanctions that could well be imposed privately against the school; these private sanctions will be discussed in detail in the next chapter.

Despite all this, there have been a number of schools in the South whose administrations, whether bravely or temerariously or with indifference to possible consequences, have already admitted students of both the white and colored races. Spring Hill College in Mobile, Alabama, is an example.[44] The parochial schools of Louisiana will be integrated at an as yet unannounced time in the future.[45] Others which have already admitted Negroes to formerly all-white institutions include Vanderbilt University, Southern Methodist University, Barry College of Miami, Florida, and Columbia Theological Seminary of Decatur, Georgia, as well as colleges in all Southern states except Mississippi and South Carolina.[46]

It is particularly noteworthy that private colleges or universities have been desegregated in all states that have specific statutory enactments designed to prevent racial integration. Thus, the initial reaction of state law enforce-

44. Spring Hill College is controlled and operated by the Roman Catholic church.
45. See the monthly *Southern School News* for data on the situation in Louisiana. On August 5, 1956, Archbishop Rummel announced that integration would be postponed until at least September, 1957. He also indicated that integration, when it comes, will be gradual, affecting the elementary parochial schools one grade at a time. The Atlanta *Constitution*, August 6, 1956, p. 1.
46. The list of former all-white schools, both public and private, which have announced that race will no longer be a condition of admission, contains only colleges and universities; it includes seventy-three private and eighty-five public institutions in the District of Columbia and seventeen states considered to constitute the South. All states except Mississippi and South Carolina are represented by at least one integrated school.

ment officials is to ignore the statutes and to allow the institutions to continue free from official sanctions. The reasons for this failure to act would indeed be interesting, but probably beyond ascertainment. Possibly the difficulties being experienced over the public schools have been enough to fully occupy the time of the officials; possibly there is no desire on their part to harass the private schools. Whether this attitude and failure to act will continue is, of course, unknown and unknowable. The statutes do exist in those states mentioned above; the opportunity for causing major trouble to the private school administration is present. What can be said at this time is little more than that the problems involved in official sanctions have not, as yet, been fully resolved.

CHAPTER THREE

PRIVATE SANCTIONS AGAINST INTEGRATION

LAW, WHETHER CREATED by legislature (law as statute) or by court (law as decision), is but one of the means by which the affairs of society are ordered, even though it may be, as Roscoe Pound maintains,[1] the most important of the numerous methods of social control. The behavior patterns of people are created or altered as a result of a congeries of factors and influences. Law at best has but a limited role to play in this process. Accordingly, there are factors other than the governmental sanctions discussed in Chapter Two that will be influential in the decision whether to mix the white and colored races in a private school. It is the purpose of this chapter to indicate the nature of these other factors and to illustrate with concrete examples the form they can take.

In order to do that, we must perforce take off our legal spectacles and replace them with those labeled "sociology." And it will be one of the basic concepts of sociology—that of social control—that will occupy our attention.

Social control is a concept that is concerned with human conduct and the manner in which it is shaped or altered.

---

[1] Pound's views are set out in his *Social Control Through Law* (1942). See also Pound, "The Lawyer as a Social Engineer," 3 *Journal of Public Law* 292 (1954).

It is "a collective term for those processes, planned or unplanned, by which individuals are taught, persuaded, or compelled to conform to the usages or life-values of groups. . . . Social control takes place when a person is induced or forced to act according to the wishes of others, whether or not in accordance with his own wishes."[2] Its purposes are "to bring about conformity, solidarity, and continuity of a particular group or society."[3]

Viewed thus, the concept has importance to our present inquiry. The relevant questions requiring discussion are: What are the nonlegal sanctions that might be visited upon the personnel of a private school considering racial integration? What are the deprivations that might be imposed upon such personnel? What, to put it another way, are the rewards to be gained by not violating the custom of a community? Are there sanctions that may be used as a countervailing force by those against whom social pressure is brought? The context in which the discussion may best be made is the pattern of practices in Negro-white relations throughout the South in the period of time since the decision in the *Segregation Cases* in May, 1954.

THE OVER-ALL PATTERN

There are two factors particularly evident in the present-day South: (1) the overwhelming majority of the Southern whites are committed, in greater or lesser degree, to continue the patterns of racial separation that have long prevailed; (2) there is a split, deep and growing, between the two communities, white and colored, so that

---
2. Roucek (editor), *Social Control* 3 (1947).
3. Young, *Sociology* 898 (1942).

any attempt to bring about a rational solution to the segregation problems seem to be foredoomed to failure. By a "rational" solution I mean one that is taken in the ideal democratic manner: full and free discussion and argument of the issues, a full airing of all the pertinent facts, and then a decision made in which all concur without serious reservation. Rationality in decision-making presupposes, however, basic agreement in end values. But that is precisely what is lacking here. In other words, the conflict is one over ends, not means.

The views of the white Southerners have been widely publicized and need no restatement here.[4] Similarly, the views of the colored minority, while not so broadly disseminated, are well known.[5]

Opposition to the law created by the Supreme Court in the *Segregation Cases* and subsequent decisions has taken two main forms. Chief and best known of these are the governmental actions of a number of Southern legislatures and the public statements of Southern politicians and community leaders. So-called "private school" plans

4. It is undoubtedly true that the South generally and the white Southerner in particular has received a "bad press" from non-Southern newspapers and magazines. This has traditionally been true, and it remains one of the chief valid criticisms that Southerners make of "yankees." For restrained statements of the Southern viewpoint, all made from different points of view, see the following articles by leading Southern newspapermen: McKnight, "Troubled South: Search for a Middle Ground," *Collier's* June 22, 1956, p. 25; McGill, "The Angry South," *Atlantic Monthly*, April, 1956, p. 31; Waring, "The Southern Case Against Desegregation," *Harper's Magazine*, January, 1956, p. 39; Carter, "Racial Crisis in the Deep South," *Saturday Evening Post*, December 17, 1956, p. 26.

5. A recent statement made by a leader of the NAACP is Hill, "The South in Conflict," *The New Leader*, April 2, 1956, p. 3. The monthly *Southern School News* is one of the best sources of statements of Negro and white alike.

and resolutions of interposition and nullification[6] have been the principal expressions of the legislatures, led by the governors and other public figures. The other type of opposition has been the actions of individuals or groups of white Southerners, acting as private citizens, aimed at imposing deprivations (or withholding rewards or benefits) upon anyone, white or colored, who favored racial integration and who worked for the implementation of the Court decision. This action, not so highly publicized as the other, is the focus of our present attention.

Much of the imposition of nonlegal sanctions upon those who incur the displeasure of the white supremacist is done *sub rosa*. Accordingly, there has been nothing more than sporadic reporting in newspapers and other media of isolated instances of this type of activity. It is, as a consequence, not known whether this action of embittered white against Negro or white "nigger-lover" is taken in concert throughout the South or is an unconnected series of operations taken by individuals or groups of individuals acting without central direction or control. On the basis of what evidence there is, however, it would appear that nonlegal sanctions have, at times at least, a state-wide operation. And there is at least a loose liaison, if not a clear tie, between groups in different states.[7]

The ability of the white Southerner to impose nonlegal pressures stems predominantly from the superior power

6. A thorough discussion of interposition and nullification may be found in a group of articles entitled, "The Doctrine of Interposition: A Round Table," 5 *Journal of Public Law* 1 (1956).

7. A loose-knit organization including groups from eleven states, known as the Federation for Constitutional Government, was formed in December, 1955. Apparently, however, local groups have almost complete autonomy. See *Southern School News*, February, 1956, p. 8, for an account of the Federation.

position of the white man in the South. The social structure is completely oriented toward patterns of white domination. Most, if not all, of the important governmental posts, judicial as well as executive and legislative, are occupied not only by white men but by those whose preferences clearly lie with the maintenance of the status quo before May, 1954. Both the Negro and the minority of the white Southerners who espouse his cause are in the same position of power-inferiority vis-à-vis the white supremacist of whatever stripe.

This fact has great significance in the manner in which the social structure is maintained or altered. Those who would create difficulties for the Negro and his champions are in the most advantageous position to do so. Mentioned in Chapter Two was one example of this: the ability of designated law enforcement officials to take action, while ostensibly only doing their duty according to the law, so as to harass or otherwise molest or annoy anyone who incurred their displeasure. Since it can be forecast with some certainty that nonlegal "private" sanctions will be invoked against some or all of those who are temerarious enough to mix the races in a private school in the South, the superior power position of those who could invoke the sanctions will make it easy for them to do so.

Historically, sporadically-imposed physical sanctions have been one of the principal means used in the South to keep the Negro "in his place" in the Southern caste system. These have included the occasional (but greatly diminishing) use of extermination (lynching and the shooting of "uppity" Negroes) and of physical punishment (such as floggings) as well as the entire set of taboos and social conventions in some or all of the South. In addition, other forms of terrorism and physical action such as wrecking buildings and burning homes have taken place from time to time. The pattern was one of a background of occasional intimidation and violence, put into operation just often enough to insure that the mass of colored people kept quiescent. Other sanctions traditionally used included those of education (the lack of it, i.e., the failure to accord even "equal" educational opportunities to that given whites) and pressures to prevent use of the ballot.[8] There has been, in addition, a variety of means to keep the Negro in a position of economic subservience so that all but a few were poor and could obtain only menial jobs.

It should not be thought that the attitude of the Southern white to the Negro has been wholly one of antagonism. So long as the Negro stayed in his place and did not try to participate in activities thought to be exclusively white, so long as he maintained an air of respect toward the whites, so long as he maintained residential separation, so long, that is to say, as he did not threaten the status of the white man, the Negro was often treated with kindness and even respect. The two communities could, and did, live very well together, and the caste system did operate so long as the Negro maintained attitudes of respect toward the white and did not give vent to any of his grievances. And often, in numerous individual instances, there was genuine liking and friendship between white and colored. Even Jim Crowism, as C. Vann Wood-

---

8. Recognition of the potency of the vote was made soon after the Civil War and steps were immediately taken to prevent Negroes from voting. Many of these have been carried down to the present.

ward has demonstrated,[9] came relatively late. The point is that rigid separation in important activities and complete exclusion from much of the community life did not prevent a large amount of interchange between the races.

The Ku Klux Klan was the chief instrumentality of the organized form of Negro repression, although as John Cash has related in his classic *The Mind of the South*[10] there were numerous examples of unorganized, individual acts of violence. The robe, the mask, and the burning cross were the symbols that for many years struck terror in the hearts of Negores and other minority groups.

In recent years, however, the Klan has suffered a major decline in importance and influence. A number of states have enacted laws aimed at hampering its activities; anti-mask laws are an example.[11] It has been placed upon the list of subversive organizations maintained by the Attorney General of the United States.[12] "Ineptly led, unmasked by state laws, and inhibited by the unfriendly attentions of the Federal Bureau of Investigation, it is a 'fringe' group in the full meaning of the term."[13]

With the decline, though not the final death, of the Klan as an important factor in racial relations, a number of other resistance groups have been formed since May, 1954. At least fifty of these organizations now exist throughout the South, and there are undoubtedly more. Although not necessarily affiliated these groups have sufficiently

9. See Woodward, *The Strange Career of Jim Crow* (1955).
10. Cash's book, published in 1941, is basic to an understanding of the South.
11. A brief discussion of anti-Klan legislation may be found in Note, 1 *Journal of Public Law* 182 (1952).
12. 5 Code of Federal Regulations § 210, App. A (1949).
13. Fleming, "Resistance Movements and Racial Desegregation," 304 *Annals* 44 (March, 1956).

identical aims and purposes to be given a common generic name—White Citizens' Councils (WCC)—and may be treated as a common organization.[14] There common denominator is opposition to desegregation, although many of them have anti-Semitic features.

Thus far at least, the WCC do not operate in the manner that led to the virtual demise of the KKK. Their membership has been publicized, their activities carried out relatively openly, there has been no use of hoods or burning crosses attributable to the WCC, and they have emphasized their intention to work "by peaceful and legal means." Their purposes and declaration of intentions may be learned from the constitution of the Association of Citizens' Councils of South Carolina:

> Its purposes are the gathering, discussion, and dissemination of information relative to the operation of constitutional government and the preservation of State sovereignty and bi-racial society, the betterment of relations between the races, the maintenance of peace, good order, and domestic tranquillity in the community, the education of the public generally thereabouts, the association with other groups having similar aims, and the doing and performance of all acts and things incident to the attainment of its purposes.[15]

Although only recently formed, they have already gained a considerable membership and exercise a significant influence over governmental activity in a number of states. This may, of course, be attributable to the fact that quasi-official support is given the WCC in some states through

---

14. A listing, doubtless incomplete, may be found in McKay, " 'With All Deliberate Speed': A Study of School Desegregation," 31 *New York University Law Review* 991 (1956).

15. Quoted at McKay, *supra* note 14, at 1065.

the active membership of high government officials.¹⁶ In less than two years after formation, the WCC in Mississippi had 300 chapters and more than 80,000 members. Alabama's groups claim more than 65,000 adherents and South Carolina's more than 55 chapters.

The WCC thus form a loose organization of Southerners willing to take strong, perhaps extreme, measures to preserve their traditional social structure and ways of doing things. Although they have not enlisted a majority of white Southerners in their ranks, still they have many important government figures and many other community leaders. The WCC, accordingly, are in a position to invoke many of the informal means of social control and thus force, or attempt to force, adherence to their preferences in racial relations. "Even critics of the WCC will concede that many of the leaders of the movement have community status in terms of political influence, economic power, or both."¹⁷ Hodding Carter, one of the more astute observers of Southern life, has said that "by and large, the men who thus far have led the Councils' movement have standing in their communities. They are, primarily, men with an obsession—namely, that integration of the public schools means blood integration as well—and this obsession is shared by many who abhor the Councils."¹⁸

TYPES OF NONLEGAL SANCTIONS

For purposes of description, the sanctions that might be

16. Such well-known political figures as Senators Eastland of Mississippi and Thurmond of South Carolina, Governor Griffin of Georgia, and Congressmen Davis of Georgia and Williams of Mississippi, among many others, indicate the pattern that is taking place.
17. Fleming, *supra* note 13, at 47.
18. Carter, "A Wave of Terror Threatens the South," *Look*, March 22, 1955.

invoked by individuals or groups in efforts to prevent change in racial patterns may be classified in three groups: physical, economic, and psychological. These control measures operate without the overt intervention of state authority; they are privately invoked by individuals and groups whose aim it is to preserve the status quo. It should be noted that although these pressures are applied privately, nevertheless they are not disturbed by state authority and thus may be said to be condoned, if not encouraged, by state officials.

Physical Sanctions

The concept of social control includes the utilization of techniques that both punish and reward. However, physical sanctions can only be applied to penalize or punish, never to reward. Thus they are essentially negative in character. And while they are doubtless the most simple and direct of the methods of social control, no doubt they are also the least frequently used. Such sporadic resort to physical punishment as does exist, however, makes it necessary to indicate the forms it can take.

Mob violence is perhaps the most spectacular example, although it is seldom resorted to. The spectacular, highly publicized action of the mob in Tuscaloosa, Alabama, following the enrollment of Autherine Lucy in the University of Alabama highlights a recent instance of racial disturbance. But while some of these actions can be expected from time to time, they should not be exaggerated. Rioting and other forms of mob violence will likely be local in nature and of relatively short duration. No government can tolerate such activities, which represent a breakdown of law and order, even if law enforcement officials are basically in agreement with the rioters.

Other physical sanctions are, in like manner, likely to be imposed only locally and sporadically, if at all, and then only by members of the lunatic fringe. They include possible extermination of the offending person or of the person who is believed to be an offender (the Till episode in Mississippi is an example, but that is merely the most sensational; a few Negroes have been killed in other parts of the South[19]); bombings of homes and meeting places (these seem to occur in connection with Negro attempts to move into white residential areas; similar episodes of this type have taken place in Chicago and Detroit, among other Northern cities); and physical punishment (an occasional flogging or beating).

All of these examples of physical sanctions that have been used aim at preventing change in social relations, and all are based on the individual's fear of physical pain or injury. They are effective only so far as an individual allows his fear to control his actions. Since, however, they are local and sporadic, their importance should not be overemphasized. This sanction in short, is of relatively minor and diminishing importance. Those who have forecast "a reign of terror" in the South are building on very flimsy evidence.

Economic Sanctions

Of more importance are the economic sanctions that have been and are being imposed to influence the conduct

---

19. For example, the Reverend George W. Lee, a Negro minister, was slain in Belzoni, Mississippi, allegedly for "activities in the NAACP and seeking voting rights for Negroes." *Southern School News*, April, 1956, p. 11.

of Negroes and their supporters. Two quotations from Southern newspapers indicate that the principal weapon of the WCC has been "economic pressure"—a euphemism for a practice that a Southern editor called "economic thuggery." The Jackson, Mississippi, *Clarion-Ledger* carried the following statement of one Fred Jones: "We can accomplish our purposes largely with economic pressure in dealing with members of the Negro race who are not cooperating, and with members of the white race who fail to cooperate, we can apply social and political pressure."[20] And at an organizing rally of the WCC in Alabama, an account of which was carried in the Montgomery, Alabama, *Advertiser*, a speaker gave blunt voice to the principle of economic coercion: "The white population in this county controls the money, and this is an advantage that the council will use to legally maintain complete segregation of the races. We intend to make it difficult, if not imposssible, for any Negro who advocates desegregation to find and hold a job, get credit or renew a mortgage."[21]

The numerous instances of economic pressure that have been reported—no doubt many, perhaps the majority, are not publicized—do not measure the influence such control actions have. They are intended as object lessons, and are designed not only to penalize the individual victim but also to intimidate and silence other potential dissenters. Thus, the action of the New Orleans Chamber of Commerce in firing the editor of its news bulletin for belonging to an anti-segregation organization is of the type of economic pressure that has wider ramifications.[22] It would

20. Quoted in Fleming, *supra* note 13, at 48.   21. *Ibid.*
22. The organization is the Southern Conference Educational Fund. *Southern School News*, May, 1956, p. 12.

make other members of the group raise serious questions about making public statements concerning the desirability of desegregation. To some extent, the use of economic reprisals has resulted in the creation of an atmosphere of fear and of refusal to "stick one's neck out." The technique has been widely used:

> Negro teachers have been discharged, Negro farmers have been denied credit, and Negro merchants have been boycotted by wholesale distributors. In a number of instances, signers of desegregation petitions directed to local school boards have recanted after their names and addresses were published by the newspapers. In a few cases, white persons believed to hold unorthodox racial views have been 'advised' by organized groups of their neighbors to move; and a small but growing number of white ministers have lost their pulpits because of their opinions on segregation.[23]

Nevertheless, economic pressure is a technique which can be used by the Negro also; it is a knife which can, and has, cut two ways. That the nonlegal sanction can be used as a weapon to fight segregation is evident from the well-known bus boycotts in Montgomery, Alabama, and Tallahassee, Florida, as well as a host of quiet, unpublicized similar movements by the Negro. The growing economic power of the Negro, in the South and in other areas of the nation, make it possible for him to exert pressure of his own. Representing more than ten percent of the population, the Negroes could hold the power of economic life or death over many small retail merchants as well as other business enterprises. Witness, for example, the advice given by a NAACP official in South Carolina, with reference to the desire of Negroes for equal seating facilities at a city-owned baseball park: "Put up your money, get a

---
23. Fleming, *supra* note 13, at 49.

lawyer and go to court.... Money is the white man's god. Any time you cut him where he feels it, he'll give in. Spend your money with your friends whether they are white or Negro. If they show themselves unfriendly with you, then go spend it with your friends elsewhere."[24]

Psychological Sanctions

The final method of social control that has been used in the South is the psychological sanction. It is probably the most important of the three we have discussed, although the other two are far more spectacular and get far more publicity. Of major importance to an individual is his status in the group in which he lives and conducts his affairs; loss of that status can be a severe, even traumatic personal experience. The psychological sanction is the one that is probably first imposed, and it is only after it has apparently failed that economic or physical sanctions are put into use.[25] Its success is dependent upon the value an individual places upon his status in his community (the sociologist's "status group").

Social ostracism—the failure to include a transgressing individual in the activities he normally considers himself a part of—is a ready example. It is, of course, a sanction that in the South would be available for use against the nonconforming white, not the Negro who already has been ostracized. The taunts and jeers of his former friends is another example, as is the vile verbal abuse that could be heaped upon him publicly. The action of the State Board

24. *Southern School News*, June, 1956, p. 14. See Gordon, "Boycotts Can Cut Two Ways," 11 *New South* No. 4, p. 5 (April, 1956): Fleming, *supra* note 13, at 49.
25. An account of the various techniques of social control may be found in LaPiere, *A Theory of Social Control*, ch. 9 (1954).

of Education, which stripped from Dr. Guy H. Wells his honorary title of president emeritus of the Georgia State College for Women, is still another example. This was done because of his activities in the promotion of interracial cooperation.[26] (The concurrent attempt to prohibit pension payments to Wells, rejected as unconstitutional by the trustees of the state retirement system, is an instance of the failure of an attempted economic sanction.)

Other psychological sanctions are threats of economic reprisal, of physical punishment, and of the loss of social "face." They thus combine with the other types of sanctions. An indication of the form threats may take can be seen in the use of the burning cross and other similarly crude but suggestive devices calculated to create terror or fear of incipient action.

AN EVALUATION

Considerable attention has been devoted to the problem of nonlegal sanctions invoked in racial matters because they make up a good part of the context in which a private school administrator operates. As Archbishop Rummel of the Roman Catholic church in Louisiana has experienced,

26. *Southern School News*, April, 1956, p. 7. Compare the following: " 'Our Southland,' said John Howard O'Dowd to his fellow South Carolinians, 'is becoming a place where nonconcurrence with the established orthodoxy is cause for rejection and social ostracism.' An editor of the Florence, S. C. *Morning News* . . . O'Dowd knew whereof he spoke. Because he had broken 'the established orthodoxy' by calling for moderation on the desegregation issue, O'Dowd was pressured into dropping the whole subject of racial integration from the *New's* editorial page. Nevertheless, threats against O'Dowd and his family and pressure on the newspaper . . . only increased. Last week Jack O'Dowd resigned 'for my own good and the good of the paper.' Next month he will join the staff of the Chicago *Sun-Times* as a reporter. Said O'Dowd regretfully: 'I'm certain that the *News* no longer will buck racial feeling.' " *Time*, July 30, 1956, p. 50.

an announced decision to integrate the races in a private school can have important results in the furor of opposition stirred up. Of course, the Catholic school in Louisiana occupies a much more important position in the educational picture than does the private school elsewhere. But the pattern could well be the same.

The private school administrator deciding whether to admit Negro students would have to ponder the possible effect that action would have on his school. Economic pressure could well be invoked against the administrator and against the school itself. Psychological sanctions could likewise result.

That this is not a fear lightly to be considered is indicated by recent actions of private school trustees in Oklahoma and North Carolina. In Oklahoma, the headmaster of the Casady private day school resigned after the board of trustees rejected an application for admission of an 11-year-old Negro boy. The trustees of the school announced that the headmaster had disagreed with the trustees on segregation barriers, recommending that they be removed at once. But the trustees felt the school's finances would suffer if it moved "too fast" on the integration issue. The school is "financed entirely on tuition and private appropriations," the trustees said, "and we felt we would approach the integration issue cautiously."[27] The school is sponsored by the Episcopal church but supported by laymen. In North Carolina, the trustees of Gardner-Webb College, a Baptist institution, decided against admitting any Negro students, saying: "Because the preponderant majority of the constituency of Gardner-Webb College reporting their opinion in the survey conducted by

27. *Southern School News*, July, 1956, p. 8.

a special committee appointed for the purpose were decidedly against the admission of Negro students and because the college cannot operate without their wholehearted support and because the student body was substantially divided on the problem, we as a board of trustees express as our opinion that we are not ready for the admission of Negroes."[28]

Nevertheless, as noted in Chapter Two, a rather large number of private schools have integrated their student bodies or have announced their intention of doing so in the near future. Significant as this is, it should not be thought of as indicative of a general pattern. Even in those schools that have admitted Negroes, the numbers involved are very small. In the public schools that have admitted Negroes, largely following court orders, there have been only a handful of colored students who have actually enrolled; the same holds true for the private school. The conclusion to be drawn is that denominational and other private schools will undoubtedly proceed with a great deal of caution before further announcements of racial integration are made and certainly before any large number of Negroes are admitted to any single school.

28. *Southern School News*, March, 1956, p. 10.

CHAPTER FOUR

THE PUBLIC NATURE OF PRIVATE EDUCATION

IT IS CLEAR THAT THE public school administrators are not the only educators who are deeply concerned with racial discrimination; some of their colleagues in private and denominational schools also face serious problems. Of course these are of a different type, being concerned for the most part with the reaction that may take place in the wake of a private school's decision to integrate the races in its student body. The private school administrator has not had to grapple with problems of imposed integration; his have been or will be voluntarily shouldered. Suppose, however, the decision is made by the Negroes (or other racial or religious group) to attempt to extend the principle of the *Segregation Cases* into nonpublic education. Suppose, in other words, there is an attempt made to break down existing racial barriers to admission in private schools. Would such an attempt succeed? A development of this as yet nonexistent but nevertheless foreseeable[1] problem area will be made in this chapter.

1. Compare the attempt, discussed in Chapter Five, to break down the racial barriers at Girard College, a private school in Philadelphia. Compare, also, the Fair Education Practices Acts of New York and New Jersey, for an account of which see Note, 64 *Harvard Law Review* 307 (1950).

In 1956 a determined effort was made to require all members of the Association of American Law Schools to eliminate racial barriers to ad-

That this problem is more than an academic one is evident from the apparent over-all program of the Negro. Their aspirations seem to include attainment of full and complete status in the social structure and not merely the elimination of official acts of discrimination, although those acts are the focal point of present-day attacks. "Integration" may be considered a concept that connotes a good deal more than merely commingling whites and nonwhites in the same public schools. Not solely formal equality of treatment by official bodies and governmental institutions but full and complete participation in all societal institutions, both those labeled "public" and those termed "private," may be considered the goal. The Negro in the United States has not in the past and does not now want equality of a form of society and way of life peculiar to his race. He wants a more equal position with full status in white culture and complete participation in white institutions.[2] "What the Negro wants is first-class citizen-

---

mission. A policy of nonsegregation was to be made a condition of becoming or remaining a member. The Association includes both private and public law schools. The attempt was defeated in a close vote at the 1955 convention of the Association. For an account of this attempt to desegregate private as well as public schools, see Ass'n of American Law Schools, *1955 Proceedings* 240-71 (1956).

2. In now famous legal language, the Negro does not want "separate but equal" treatment in any important activity. See Logan (editor), *What the Negro Wants* (1944) for statements of Negro leaders of the aspirations of the American colored citizens. In Rowan, "What Do Negroes Really Want?" *Look*, April 3, 1956, p. 34, a leader of the Louisiana NAACP is quoted as follows: "Many years ago, we asked for school equalization. Then, we couldn't get it; now we don't want it. We want nothing less than total integration in all facets of American life—and we won't stop until we get it."

In the same article, a Negro teacher is quoted as follows: "There is nothing complicated about what we want. We just want the same things other Americans want—the same opportunities, rights and responsibilities."

See also Richardson, "What the Negro Wants," 11 *New South* No. 1, p. 8 (January, 1956).

ship without any reservations. He wants nothing not compatible with democracy and the Constitution. On the contrary, his demand is that he share equally in American democracy under the Constitution and participate fully in American life."[3]

It appears, further, that the Negro movement in the United States is, when viewed in perspective, part of a world-wide movement by colored peoples for status. In other countries it takes the form of anti-colonialism and nationalism, of violence and strife; here it takes the form of achieving goals through the use of legal tactics and strategy in a constitutional framework. But the aim is the same, even though there are no outward identifications made between different national groups and no verbalization of the essential identity of interest. "The thoughtful American Negro," it has been said, "shares with almost all the other colored peoples of the world a desire to improve the status of his people in relation to the white race."[4]

It is, accordingly, not fanciful to raise and discuss the question of possible attempts to open the doors of private education. At some time in the future the private school administrator is likely to have to meet the problem head on.

Moving as he does through legal channels, the Negro

---

3. Davie, *Negroes in American Society* 455 (1949). Despite the statement quoted in the text, no systematic survey of the aspirations of the Negroes has been made. The statements of Negro leaders are available, but they are usually couched in generalities so that it is difficult to ascertain the Negro position on any particular issue. The problem is one that cries out for careful analysis and exploration, as is its other side: the problem of learning exactly what it is the white man fears or dislikes in the Negro. Some exact knowledge of the facts in both areas should help displace some of the emotion and extreme statements usually heard.

4. Article entitled "The American Negro" in the London *Times*, July 23, 1952, page 7. See van der Post, *The Dark Eye in Africa* (1955).

can choose between two alternatives in his pursuit of improved social status: he can attempt to have legislation enacted or he can go to court and try for favorable judicial reaction. His choice will undoubtedly be conditioned by the state in which the action is brought. For example, in New York a successful movement in the legislature has resulted in the enactment of a Fair Educational Practices Act.[5] This statute, which is a part of the series of New York statutes designed to combat discrimination in privately owned and operated establishments, makes it illegal to discriminate on the basis of race, color, or religion in the admission of students to private schools. Other states have statutes that, even before the decision in the *Segregation Cases*, forbade racial discrimination.[6]

The main focus of the Negro has, however, been in the judiciary. Recognizing the complete impossibility of getting any favorable legislation enacted in even the border states, to say nothing of the deep South, the courts and the judicial process have been resorted to. And it has been the federal, not the state, courts that have been the primary vehicle, for ultimately it is the federal Constitution that is invoked in aid of the demand for equality.[7] Ultimately, also, it will be the United States Supreme Court that will

[5.] This act is modeled on the Fair Employment Practices Acts that several states have enacted. The New York statute has the following declaration of policy: "It is hereby declared to be the policy of the state that the American ideal of equality of opportunity requires that students, otherwise qualified, be admitted to educational institutions without regard to race, color, religion, creed or national origin. . . ." For a discussion of this and similar statutes, see Note, 64 *Harvard Law Review* 307 (1950).

[6.] These statutes are collected in Murray, *States' Laws on Race and Color* (1950) (with a 1955 supplement).

[7.] It is for more than political reasons, that the Supreme Court, not Congress, has been the vehicle used by the Negro: Congress, under existing interpretation, has no authority to legislate in the field of racial relations.

be called upon to make the authoritative pronouncement should a movement to open private education be made. Would that Court, under existing and foreseeable legal doctrine and constitutional interpretation, extend the principle of nondiscrimination to encompass all education?

THE CONSTITUTIONAL CONCEPT OF "STATE ACTION"

We can start with the *Segregation Cases* themselves and with some of the language used by Chief Justice Warren. An important part of the decision, derived not from express language but as a gloss from the entire opinion, is the Court's finding of a national interest in education and in the development of the child over and above the concern of the parents and of the local community. The Chief Justice made statements that are perhaps the most extreme yet uttered by the Court on the subject of education:

> [We recognize] the importance of education to our democratic society.
>
> . . . .
>
> [Education] is required in the performance of our most basic public responsibilities, even service in the armed forces.
>
> . . . .
>
> [Education] is the very foundation of good citizenship. Today it is a principal instrument in awakening the child to cultural values, in preparing him for later professional training, and in helping him to adjust normally to his environment. In these days, it is doubtful that any child may reasonably be expected to succeed in life if he is denied the opportunity of an education.[8]

Language such as this buttresses the view that the societal interest in education overrides and transcends the

---

8. The quoted statements are taken from Brown v. Board of Education, 347 U.S. 483 (1954). Compare School District v. Alamance County, 211 N.C. 213 (1937) in which the Supreme Court of North Carolina characterized education as a "sacred duty" of the state.

interests of the parents as well as those of the child. The Court, in using the language, has made an important recognition of a concept that may have far-reaching ramifications. It is possible that it has created the basis for mounting an attack on the citadel of private learning. Does the finding of a national interest in education, when added to the further finding that enforced racial segregation generates feelings of inferiority in the objects of discrimination, suggest that it is a logical step to require integration wherever education is carried on?[9]

It is difficult to forecast what the Supreme Court will do with a case once it is before it. In the absence of a concrete factual situation out of which the legal and constitutional question has been posed, prediction of a possible future decision is often erroneous. It is possible, however, to discuss the problem area, to point out lines of development in the past, and to attempt an extrapolation. What obstacles would an attempt to force the doors of private education open have to surmount? The chief roadblock is the language of the Constitution itself and an almost unbroken line of interpretation since 1872. The pertinent part of the Constitution is the Fourteenth Amendment and its provision that "[no] State [shall] deprive any person of life, liberty or property, without due process of law; nor deny to any person within its jurisdiction the equal protection of the laws. . . ."

The key word is "state," for it is on this word that the concept of state action finds its source and its validity. The Constitution, it is often said, "runs against governments

---

9. Such a fear has been expressed. See Valenti, Woefl & Shaughnessy, "A Double Revolution? The Supreme Court's Desegregation Decision," 25 *Harvard Education Review* 1 (1955). The authors are members of the faculty of Loyola University in Chicago.

only." Thus, those who would break down the barriers in private education must present a factual situation from which it will be possible for the justices of the Supreme Court to draw the conclusion that the state is somehow intimately involved in privately-controlled education. In the *Slaughterhouse Cases*,[10] decided in 1872 by the Supreme Court, it was said that the restrictions of the Fourteenth Amendment apply only to the actions of state governments and do not apply either to private individuals or to private institutions. Since that time there has been an evolutionary development of state action. The result is that today it is possible to predict with fair accuracy whether a particular factual situation so involves a state as to bring it within the purview of the Fourteenth Amendment. So far as education is concerned, the short answer is that the Court has not extended the concept of state action to include anything more than what is publicly controlled; nor, to hazard a guess, is it likely that it would now or in the immediate future. However, it has been said that the "Court has shown that the concept of private action must yield to a conception of state action where public functions are being performed."[11] Hence, this inquiry.

One Line of Judicial Development

It is, as noted above, action *by the state* that is prohibited by the Fourteenth Amendment when such action deprives a person of due process of law or denies him equal protection of the laws. But the Supreme Court has never drawn a precise and definitive line between what is official (state) action and what is purely private. How-

10. 36 U.S. (16 Wall.) (1872).
11. Freund, "Umpiring the Federal System," in MacMahon (editor), *Federalism: Mature and Emergent* 159, 162 (1955).

ever, it has consistently held to the requirement that action (or nonaction, in some cases) by some official or by some organ of the state is a necessary prerequisite to setting the Fourteenth Amendment in motion. In the *Civil Rights Cases*[12] in 1883, Mr. Justice Bradley stated that "it is state action of a particular character that is prohibited. Individual invasion of individual rights is not the subject matter of the amendment." But even before this the Court had already extended the Amendment to actions of individuals exercising state powers, whether they were following state law or not.[13] Thus the Amendment applies to more than statutes and the actions of state officials in compliance with statutes. Later on the Court went even further and held that acts of state officials, not only when unauthorized by state law but also when prohibited by it, were within the purview of the Amendment.[14]

Thus the concept of state action has been an expanding one, which apparently has not yet completed its evolution. Two parallel lines of development are discernible: (1) that noted above in which action by any state official or by any organ of the state performing state duties has been found to fall within the concept of state action, and (2) that in which the concept has been found to apply to officials and organizations that have no direct connection with the state but exercise functions similar to those of the state. In both these lines of development may be seen the tendency of the Court to bring more and more under the

12. 109 U.S. 3, 11 (1883).
13. Ex parte Virginia, 100 U.S. 339 (1879).
14. See, for example, Home Tel. & Tel. Co. v. Los Angeles, 227 U.S. 278 (1913); Raymond v. Chicago Union Traction Co., 207 U.S. 20 (1907). Consult Hale, "Unconstitutional Acts as Federal Crimes," 60 *Harvard Law Review* 65, 78-90 (1946).

tent of state action. Whether this is the camel's nose soon to be followed by the entire animal remains to be seen.

There are several cases that have added to the doctrinal development of the concept. In *Virginia v. Rives*,[15] a case involving exclusion of Negroes from the jury in a trial of a Negro for murder, Mr. Justice Field uttered the following relevant language in a concurring opinion:

> If an executive or judicial officer exercises power with which he is not invested by law, and does unauthorized acts, the State is not responsible for them. The action of the judicial officer in such a case, where the rights of a citizen under the laws of the United States are disregarded, may be reviewed and corrected or reversed by [the Supreme Court]: it cannot be imputed to the State, so as to make it evidence that she in her sovereign or legislative capacity denies the rights invaded, or refuses to allow their enforcement. It is merely the ordinary case of an erroneous ruling of an inferior tribunal. Nor can the unauthorized action of an executive office, impinging upon the rights of the citizen, be taken as evidence of her intention as policy so as to charge upon her a denial of such rights.[16]

This effort to engraft into the Constitution the normal rules of agency law—the agent acting beyond the scope of his authority cannot bind his principal—found Court cognizance and acceptance in 1904. At that time, a unanimous Court held that the action of a state administrative body, which had been taken in direct violation of a state statute, could not be state action "within the intent and meaning of the Fourteenth Amendment." In the words of Chief Justice Fuller, "it is for the state courts to remedy acts of state officers done without authority of or contrary to state law."[17]

15. 100 U.S. 313 (1879). 16. *Ibid.*, at 334.
17. Barney v. City of New York, 193 U.S. 430, 438 (1904).

But that was the last time the Court was willing to take such a position. Three years later, in *Raymond v. Chicago Union Traction Co.*,[18] it found state action in a case where a state board of tax equalization failed, contrary to the state constitution, to make a uniform property valuation for tax purposes. A violation of due process was found over the dissenting voice of Justice Holmes, who stated:

[I am] unable to grasp the principle on which the State is said to deprive the appellee of its property without due process of law because a subordinate board . . . is said to have violated the express requirement of the State in its constitution. . . . I should have thought that the action of the State was to be found in its constitution, and that no fault could be found with that until the authorized interpreter of that constitution, the Supreme Court [of the state], had said that it sanctioned the alleged wrong.

The new position of the Court was underscored in 1913 in a case which clearly refuted the earlier (and Holmes's) position:

[W]here a state officer is doing an act which could only be done upon the predicate that there was such power, the inquiry as to the repugnancy of the act to the Fourteenth Amendment cannot be avoided by insisting that there is a want of power. That is to say, a state officer cannot on the one hand as a means of doing a wrong forbidden by the Amendment proceed upon the assumption of the possession of state power and at the same time for the purposes of avoiding the application of the Amendment, deny the power and thus accomplish the wrong.[19]

To further buttress the view that action illegal under state law may still be state action are two more recent cases. In *Iowa-Des Moines National Bank v. Bennett*[20]

18. 207 U.S. 20 (1907).
19. Home Tel. & Tel. Co. v. Los Angeles, 227 U.S. 278, 288 (1913).
20. 284 U.S. 239 (1931).

the Court in 1931 found state action in a systematic discrimination by tax assessors even though the state court had held the acts to be unauthorized and thus not the action of the state. And in 1945, in *Screws v. United States*,[21] the Court again held to the view that it is "immaterial that the state officer exceeded the limits of his authority" in deciding whether state action is involved. Since the officer "acts in the name and for the State, and is clothed with the State's power, his act is that of the State." Some language by Justice Rutledge in his concurring opinion is of interest:

> It is too late now . . . to question that in these matters abuse binds the state and is its act, when done by one to whom it has given power to make the abuse effective to achieve the forbidden ends. Vague ideas of dual federalism, of ultra vires doctrine imported from private agency, do not nullify what four years of civil strife and eighty years have verified.

Similarly, the concept of state action has been expanded to include the actions of any organ of the state. The racial covenant cases provide apt illustration. *Shelley v. Kraemer*[22] in 1948 involved a racial restrictive covenant, which had been invoked when the property in question was sold to a Negro. A decree of specific performance of the covenant granted by a state court was challenged on the ground that such state court enforcement of a racial covenant was (1) state action and (2) an invalid discrimination under the equal protection clause. Although the discrimination had been started by private individuals, "but for the active participation of the state courts, supported by the full panoply of state power," the Negro

21. 325 U.S. 91 (1945).
22. 334 U.S. 1 (1948).

would have been allowed to purchase and occupy the land. The opinion by Chief Justice Vinson contained the following language, which is important to the present inquiry:

> Since the decision of this Court in the Civil Rights Cases . . . the principle has become firmly imbedded in our constitutional law that the action inhibited by the first section of the Fourteenth Amendment is only such action as may fairly be said to be that of the States. That Amendment erects no shield against merely private conduct, however discriminatory or wrongful.

Shelley was followed by *Barrows v. Jackson* in 1953, a case in which the Court said that the same principle applies to an action for damages against a party violating such a covenant by selling the land to a Negro. In the course of its opinion, to which Chief Justice Vinson strongly dissented, the Court said:

> If a state court awards damages for breach of a restrictive covenant, a prospective seller of restricted land will either refuse to sell to non-Caucasians or else will require non-Caucasians to pay a higher price to meet the damages which the seller may incur. Solely because of their race, non-Caucasians will be unable to purchase, own, and enjoy property on the same terms of Caucasians. Denial of this right by state action deprives such non-Caucasians, unidentified but identifiable, of equal protection in violation of the Fourteenth Amendment.

So far as finding state action is concerned, the Court reasoned as follows:

> . . . it becomes not [the seller's] voluntary choice, but the State's choice that she observe her covenant or suffer damages. The action of the state court at law to sanction the validity of the restrictive covenant . . . would constitute state action as surely as it was state action to enforce such covenants in equity, as in *Shelley*. . . .[23]

[23]. 346 U.S. 249 (1953). Chief Justice Vinson, dissenting, stated that "these racial restrictive covenants, whatever we may think of them, are not

When put together, *Shelley* and *Barrows* seem to add up to the proposition that racial discrimination is legal, i.e., not unlawful, when done privately, but that there is a stigma attached to it making it improper for a court to give official sanction to exercises of this legal "right." This poses a neat jurisprudential question of whether it is possible to have a right for which the possessor cannot get judicial enforcement. In other words, does not the sum of *Shelley* added to *Barrow* equal a judicial declaration of invalidity of the racial covenant?[24]

A sequel to the racial covenant cases came in 1955 in a case that will be discussed more fully in the next chapter. The case is *Charlotte Park and Recreation Comm'n v. Barringer*;[25] it involved a grant of land to a city to be used as a park for white people only, with the provision that the land was to revert to the grantor should it be used by others than whites. This provision the Supreme Court of North Carolina characterized as a fee simple determinable, and reasoned that since it operated without the intervention of the state judicial machinery (it was "automatic" said the court) no state action was involved so as to bring it within the scope of the doctrine of the *Shelley* case. The United States Supreme Court refused to review the decision.[26] Eventually, however, it will have to do so; until

---
legal nullities so far as any doctrine of federal law is concerned; it is not unlawful to make them; it is not unlawful to enforce them unless the method by which they are enforced in some way contravenes the Federal Constitution or a federal statute." *Ibid.*, at 261.

24. Cf. Huber, "Revolution in Private Law?" 6 *South Carolina Law Quarterly* 8 (1953).

25. 242 N.C. 311, 88 S.E. 2d 114 (1955).

26. The case title was changed when it was considered by the United States Supreme Court: Leeper v. Charlotte Park and Recreation Comm'n, 350 U.S. 983 (1956).

that time, the technique of the racial clause in a fee simple determinable would seem to be available for use by those who wish to avoid the impact of the racial covenant cases.

Another Line of Development

The foregoing cases, which make it clear that any action of any official or organ of a state falls within the scope of the state action concept, have not as yet been applied to situations where there is a failure to act. The reach of the Fourteenth Amendment, accordingly, is negative in that it serves to invalidate particular acts of improper action adjudged to be violative of due process or equal protection standards; it has no affirmative thrust, although the *Barrows* case may indicate a possible trend in that direction. It takes action of a state, moreover, to trigger the amendment; nonaction, i.e., passive acquiescence in unofficial discrimination, has not been proscribed, even though it is of course protected by authority of state law and state power.[27]

Nevertheless, the clear trend of judicial decision-making is to bring more and more activity within the reach

27. See, however, Pekelis, *Law and Social Action* 120-23 (1950) for an argument that state inaction can be action under the Constitution. And see Hale, "Force and the State," 35 *Columbia Law Review* 149 (1935). In Comment, 45 *Michigan Law Review* 733 (1947) the following statement appears: "What is action by the state and where it ceases is an interesting speculation in political philosophy. In a final sense, state action permeates society, for the existence of anything and the action of any individual or group is permitted, commanded or forbidden by the state: it can fairly be said that everything in the social organism takes character from its relation to the central collective purpose manifested by the government. But a distinction is made in the common understanding between action by the state and the action of private persons and it is in terms of this distinction that the Fourteenth Amendment has been held to speak. Perhaps the only logical principle on which to found the distinction is to attribute that action to the state which embodies a purpose of the government or of one entrusted with its authority which is separable from the purposes of private individuals."

of the limitations of the Constitution. Since the beginning of our national history, governments have been increasingly made subject to due process and similar limitations. At the outset, only the federal government was circumscribed by the Constitution (by the Bill of Rights); then the Civil War amendments (the Thirteenth, Fourteenth, and Fifteenth) brought the states within that circumscription; since 1865 judicial interpretation has extended the area to counties and cities and other local sovereignties. What is true in the series of cases discussed above is equally true, in a parallel line of development of the concept of state action, in the series of cases involving the application of the Constitution to what may be termed "private governments."[28] These cases involve situations where an ostensibly private organization performs acts that either are of the type normally performed by government or are of such overriding importance as to make those acts, in the language of the California Supreme Court, "quasi-public."

The voting cases (the so-called "white primary" cases) furnish instructive guidance to the length to which the Supreme Court is willing to extend the concept of state action when the activity in question is considered of vital importance. These cases have arisen and been decided under both the Fourteenth Amendment and the Fifteenth Amendment. The latter reads in pertinent part as follows: "The right of citizens of the United States to vote shall not be denied or abridged by the United States or by any State on account of race, color, or previous condition of servitude." Since the principal problem under both

---

28. "It seems to me that there is more than an a priori hypothesis to support the notion that our generation of constitutional lawyers is discovering a new dimension in our federal structure—the dimension of private governments." Pekelis, *supra* note 27, at 96.

amendments is whether state action is involved, the cases will be considered as a group with the label "white primary cases" being used generically.

Since the Civil War a practice of systematic exclusion of the Negro from the polls has characterized the South. It is only in recent years that a significant number of Negroes has gained the ballot, and even now that number is pitifully small; more, it is diminishing in some sections of the South.[29] The period has been characterized by a series of attempts by Negroes to gain full voting stature through the medium of Supreme Court invalidation of exclusion practices. The techniques used to prevent voting by Negroes have been "grandfather" clauses, educational qualifications, registration requirements, and restrictions on membership in a political party. Only the latter device concerns us here.[30]

The decisional development has been fairly uniform and has revealed a consistent trend toward the enfranchisement of the Negro. A state statute that denied Negroes the right to vote in party primary elections was held to be state action and a denial of equal protection.[31] When the Texas legislature subsequently tried to avoid the impact of

29. While there is no doubt that, over the years, there has been a marked increase in the number of Negroes voting, at the same time in such parts of the South as the so-called "black belt" the number has been decreasing since the Supreme Court's segregation decisions. See the article by Hodding Carter, "Racial Crisis in the Deep South," *Saturday Evening Post*, December 17, 1955, p. 26; O'Connor, "Negro Voter in the South," 29 *Interracial Review* No. 1, p. 9 (January, 1956).

30. In 1939 Justice Frankfurter had this to say: "The [Fifteenth] Amendment nullifies sophisticated as well as simple-minded modes of discrimination. It hits onerous procedural requirements which effectively handicap exercise of the franchise by the colored race although the abstract right to vote may remain unrestricted as to race." Lane v. Wilson, 307 U.S. 268, 275 (1939).

31. Nixon v. Herndon, 273 U.S. 536 (1927).

that decision by forming an executive committee to which it gave the power to decide on qualifications for membership in the Democratic party, the Court again struck down the legislation on the ground that the committee was an agency of the state.[32] The next attempt was to restrict membership through action of the state convention of the party; here again, although first failing to find state action,[33] the Court invalidated the restriction. The reason given was that state statutes set out performance of certain duties by party officials and made other official uses of the party machinery. "The party takes its character as a state agency from the duties imposed upon it by state statutes; the duties do not become matters of private law because they are performed by a political party."[34]

Following that decision South Carolina repealed all statutory provisions regarding primary elections and political parties; nevertheless, a requirement of the Democratic party that only white persons could vote in primary elections was declared to be invalid state action.[35] That decision, by the Court of Appeals for the Fourth Circuit, found that the act of a political party was state action "where the state law has made the primary an integral part of the procedure of choice or where in fact the primary effectively controls the choice." The political party, in other words, could not be considered a private club. And in a federal district court decision in 1948, a requirement of the Democratic party of South Carolina that white as well as Negro qualified voters, before voting in the pri-

---

32. Nixon v. Condon, 286 U.S. 73 (1932).
33. Grovey v. Townsend, 295 U.S. 45 (1935).
34. Smith v. Allwright, 321 U.S. 649, 663 (1944).
35. Rice v. Elmore, 165 F. 2d 387, 391 (C.A. 4th, 1947), cert. den. 333 U.S. 875 (1948).

mary, take an oath that they would support separation of the races was invalidated.[36] The final link came in 1953 in the *Jaybird Primary* case, *Terry v. Adams*.[37] Again, Texas provided the arena for the conflict. This time an attempt to place the primary one step further from the state was made: an organization calling itself the Jaybird Association was formed to control the designation of party nominees. Again, the Supreme Court found state action, saying that for a state "to permit such a duplication of its election processes is to permit a flagrant abuse of those processes to defeat the purposes of the Fifteenth Amendment. . . . It violates the Fifteenth Amendment for a state, by such circumvention, to permit within its borders the use of any device that produces an equivalent of the prohibited election."[38]

A comparable development of the application of due process and equal protection constitutional concepts to ostensibly private organizations is revealed in another group of cases: *Kerr v. Enoch Pratt Free Library*,[39] *Norris v. Mayor and City of Baltimore*,[40] *Dorsey v. Stuyvesant Town Corporation*,[41] *Marsh v. Alabama*,[42] and *Betts v. Easley*.[43] These cases pose squarely the problem of whether an organization traditionally and normally con-

36. Brown v. Baskin, 78 F. Supp. 933 (E.D.S.C., 1948), affirmed, 174 F. 2d 391 (C.A. 4th, 1949).
37. 345 U.S. 461 (1953).
38. *Ibid.*, at 469. Justice Minton, dissenting, stated: "Does [the] failure of the State to act to prevent individuals from doing what they have the right as individuals to do amount to state action? I venture the opinion it does not." *Ibid.*, at 489.
39. 149 F. 2d 212 (C.A. 4th, 1945), cert. den., 326 U.S. 721 (1945).
40. 78 F. Supp. 451 (D.Md., 1948).
41. 299 N.Y. 512, 87 N.E. 2d 541 (1949), cert. den., 339 U.S. 981 (1950).
42. 326 U.S. 501 (1946).
43. 161 Kan. 459, 169 P. 2d 831 (1946).

sidered to be "private" can have sufficient "public" characteristics so as to make constitutional prescriptions apply to it. The five cases do not, it should be mentioned, reach uniform results; they display all of the conflicting considerations inherent in the state action problem and all of the doubts raised in the minds of the judges reaching the decisions. Since they afford the closest existing analogy to the inquiry of this chapter, they deserve exposition in some detail.

Kerr involved a privately endowed library in Baltimore controlled by a board of trustees appointed by the original donor; however, the operating funds came mostly from the city and state. Negroes had been barred from the training school for librarians conducted by the library. This was held to be state action and, accordingly, an invalid discrimination under the equal protection clause of the Fourteenth Amendment. This case is particularly noteworthy even though it was not rendered by the United States Supreme Court: it went beyond *Smith v. Allwright* and the other voting cases in finding state action in an activity not strictly "governmental" in nature, one which, to use orthodox language, is "proprietary."[44] It would be on *Kerr* and its rationale that any concerted attempt to breach the walls of private education would be based. Hence, the following language of the Court of Appeals is important. Quoting *Nixon v. Condon*, one of the voting cases, the court said:

> ... the test is not whether the members of the [activity] are the representatives of the state in the strict sense in which an agent is the representative of his principal. The test is whether they are

---

44. The governmental-proprietary distinction is often used by judges to explain a result, particularly in cases involving municipal corporations.

to be classified as representatives of the state to such an extent and in such a sense that the great restraints of the Constitution set limits to their action.[45]

Of course it would require an extension—a major extension—of the *Kerr* case to breach the walls of private education, because the court was careful to point out the close financial connection the library had with the city of Baltimore and the fact that the city officials could and did exercise control over the library.

The *Norris* case, another arising in Baltimore, shows the importance of this factor. In that case, in an opinion noteworthy for its discussion of the judicial standards of judgment for distinguishing private from public institutions, the federal district judge stated that the "legal test between a public and private corporation is whether the corporation is subject to control by public authority, state or municipal."[46]

Dorsey v. Stuyvesant Town Corporation furnishes further instructive guidance, although that case was decided by only a four-to-three margin in the New York Court of Appeals and has since been reversed by subsequent legislation and, hence, has little value as precedent. Stuyvesant was a wholly owned subsidiary of the Metropolitan Life Insurance Company. After entering into a contract with New York City under which the city condemned land and granted a tax exemption, Stuyvesant Town was built in New York City. Under the contract, the corporation agreed to adhere to certain building standards, to permit city auditors to inspect the books, and to turn over to the city any cash surplus upon the dissolution

45. 149 F. 2d at 219.
46. 78 F. Supp. at 458.

of the corporation. Negroes sought to enjoin the corporation from leasing only to white persons, but the injunction was denied. On appeal, the four majority judges of the New York court admitted that the federal courts had held "private groups subject to the constitutional restraints when they perform functions of a governmental character in matters of great public importance." Nevertheless, they sought to distinguish the *Marsh* case (discussed below) on the ground that "the state has lent its power in support of the actions of private individuals or corporations, and in so doing has clothed the private act with the character of state action."

Although recognizing that the concept of state action is an expanding one, the four judges still felt such action had been found in the past "only in cases where the state has consciously exerted its power in aid of discrimination or where private individuals have acted in a governmental capacity so recognized by the state." If state action were to be found in the circumstances of *Dorsey*, they said:

> [It would come] perilously close to asserting that any state assistance to an organization which discriminates necessarily violates the Fourteenth Amendment. Tax exemption and the power of eminent domain are freely given to many organizations which necessarily limit their benefits to a restricted group. It has not yet been held that the recipients are subject to the restraints of the Fourteenth Amendment.

To this, the three dissenting judges vigorously maintained that "even the conduct of private individuals offends against the [equal protection clause] if it appears in an activity of public importance and if the state has accorded the transaction either the panoply of its authority or the weight of its power, interest and support."⁴⁷

Compare this language to that of the United States Supreme Court in *Marsh v. Alabama*, the so-called "company town" case. The town was Chickasaw, Alabama, wholly owned by the Gulf Shipbuilding Corporation, which had built the streets, sidewalks, and other public necessities and had maintained a privately organized and paid police and fire department system. Chickasaw looked like any other small American town. The plaintiff, a member of Jehovah's Witnesses was arrested after she refused to leave the town when ordered to do so by company officials. She was convicted under an Alabama statute that makes it a crime to remain on the property of another after being warned to leave. The conviction was reversed by the United States Supreme Court on religious freedom grounds. "The more an owner, for his advantage, opens up his property for use by the public in general," the Court said, "the more do his rights become circumscribed by the statutory and constitutional rights of those who use it."

This appears to be an explicit recognition of the notion that the Constitution can be applied to private agencies. The Court went on to say:

> Whether a corporation or a municipality owns or possesses the

47. 299 N.Y. at 542. Flack, *Adoption of the Fourteenth Amendment* 262-63 (1908) suggests that individual action was included in state action, or so was believed by many at the time the Fourteenth Amendment became a part of the Constitution. See the dissenting opinion of Justice Harlan in the Civil Rights Cases, 109 U.S. 3, 26, 57-59 (1883). In Hale, "Force and the State," 35 *Columbia Law Review* 149 (1935), it is argued that an omission by a state to enforce or secure the equal rights designed to be protected by the Fourteenth Amendment is state action. According to Hale, a state that omits to secure rights, denies them.

town, the public . . . has an identical interest in the functioning of the community in such manner that the channels of communication remain free. . . . The managers [of Chickasaw] appointed by the corporation cannot curtail the liberty of press and religion . . . consistently with the purposes of the constitutional guarantees.

Although not stated expressly, this is tantamount to the Court's saying that the Fourteenth Amendment limited the powers of the corporation owning the town—an admittedly private organization that received no help from and had no connection with the state!

The other organizations usually called private that have had constitutional limitations applied to them are labor unions. *Steele v. Louisville & Nashville Ry.*[48] foreshadowed the development. In that case the United States Supreme Court remarked:

[If the Railway Labor Act conferred an exclusive bargaining power on a union] without any commensurate statutory duty toward its members, constitutional questions arise. For the representative is clothed with powers not unlike that of a legislature which is subject to constitutional limitations on its power to deny, restrict, destroy, or discriminate against the rights of those for whom it legislates and which is also under an affirmative constitutional duty equally to protect those rights.

The Court refused to rule on this constitutional question, choosing instead to base its decision on a question of statutory interpretation, but Justice Murphy had the following to say in a concurring opinion:

While such a union is essentially a private organization, its powers to represent and bind all members of a class or craft is

---

48. 323 U.S. 192 (1944). An important extension of this came in 1956 in the case of Syres v. Oil Workers International Union, 350 U.S. 892 (1955) (doctrine of *Steele* case extended to unions certified under Taft-Hartley Act).

derived solely from Congress. The Act contains no language which directs the manner in which the bargaining representative shall perform its duties. But it cannot be assumed that Congress meant to authorize the representative to act so as to ignore rights guaranteed by the Constitution. Otherwise the Act would bear the stigma of unconstitutionality under the Fifth Amendment in this respect.

Betts v. Easley, a Kansas case, is a direct holding to that effect. In this case, a labor union designated under the Railway Labor Act as collective bargaining agent for all of the workmen involved excluded Negro workmen from full participation in the privileges available to others. Negroes were admitted only in a separate, allied organization that was "under the jurisdiction of and represented by the delegation of the nearest white local." The Supreme Court of Kansas held that this violated the Fifth Amendment's due process clause, the court saying that the union could not be regarded as a "private association of individuals free from the constitutional and statutory restraints which attach to public agencies."[49]

The United States Supreme Court, in *Brotherhood of Railroad Trainmen v. Howard,*[50] in like fashion has recognized that labor unions at times have a public character. Other state courts have followed the same course. For example, in 1944 the California Supreme Court, in a case involving a closed shop, said:

Where a union has . . . attained a monopoly of the supply of labor by means of closed shop agreements and other forms of collective labor action, such a union occupies a quasi-public position

---

49. The *Betts* case is one of several that together add up to the proposition that the limitations of the federal Constitution may, at times, run against individuals. See note 51, *infra.*

50. 343 U.S. 768 (1952).

similar to that of a public service business and it has certain corresponding obligations. It may no longer claim the same freedom from legal restraint enjoyed by golf clubs or fraternal associations. Its asserted right to choose its own members does not merely relate to social relations; it affects the fundamental right to work for a living.[51]

AN EVALUATION

Judicial construction of the constitutional concept of state action has been discussed in some detail because the concept is particularly important at this juncture of our national history. We are in the midst of an era when the Negro, long under the stigma of second-class citizenship or worse, is making determined efforts to improve his status. The assault on historical patterns of discrimination has been in serious operation only twenty years or so. During this time tremendous gains have been made, so much so that there is no doubt that official acts of discrimination if not already outlawed, will be eliminated and the Negro will have full status so far as the activities and pronouncements of formal governmental authority are concerned. But it is unlikely that he will be satisfied with mere formal equality of treatment, unless that equality is also true of the operational activities of the important societal institutions—education, for one, and what is perhaps more important, opportunity to work and earn a better living, for another.

In accomplishing this expanded goal the Negro would

51. James v. Marinship Corp., 25 Cal. 2d 721, 155 P. 2d 329 (1944). Cf. Berle, *The 20th Century Capitalist Revolution* (1954). In Note, 54 *Michigan Law Review* 567, 570 (1956), it is asserted that the results of the *Syres* case (*supra* note 48) supports "the view that a federally certified union is, in effect, a quasi-governmental agency, the actions of which are subject to the limitations of the Fifth Amendment."

have an easier legal row to hoe if he used legislation, as distinguished from judicial, action.[52] But of course legislation designed to equalize the status of Negro to white would be impossible of enactment in at least the South if not in much of the rest of the nation. Hence, judicial action would be the only feasible avenue to follow. To be successful, that action would have to be designed to get Supreme Court asquiescence in an even more expanded concept of state action than that of the past. The argument, if and when made, would run like this: the restrictive covenant, white primary, company town, and closed shop cases have shown that ostensibly private action must yield to an expanded concept of state action when important public functions are being performed; the Supreme Court in the *Segregation Cases* found a national interest in education—in other words indicated that education was an important public function; there is some state governmental subsidy of private (particularly denominational) education in the form of tax exemptions, free textbooks, bus transportation, and similar subventions; therefore— so the argument would go—the constitutional prohibitions should be held to apply to all education, whether public or nonpublic.

What would be the reaction of the Supreme Court to such an argument? Several statements may be made. First, under present doctrine the Court would undoubtedly refuse to accept the case. The reasons for this are multiple. For one, there is no reason to believe that the Supreme Court wishes to carry the doctrine of the *Segregation Cases* to its logical extreme. It is fallacious to think that

---

52. Cf. Berger, *Equality by Statute* (1952); Ruchames, *Race, Jobs, and Politics* (1953).

any principle will be projected to its logical conclusion. To think so is to express a "fear, by no means uncommon, that judges are somehow compelled by a sort of iron logical compulsion, to proceed from one conclusion to all others which might seem analogous by any syllogistic extravagance. That no such compulsion exists is the peculiar virtue of the common-law tradition."[53] The law itself can be viewed as a group of concepts that have been stopped short of an ultimate extreme. Much of law, as in all of politics, is a balancing of diverse interests; it is seldom indeed that any concept is of such overriding importance that it will be carried out without regard for countervailing interests. This is particularly true of the "great generalities" of the Constitution. The point is, there is no inherent dynamism that would make the principle of nondiscrimination encompass all education, both public and private.

Furthermore, the cases that have found judicial expansion of the concept of state action are distinguishable in part. In most, if not all, of them the activity in question (e.g., voting, earning a living, community life) not only is important to society—that is, not only is "fundamental" or "governmental"—but it has in each case no acceptable alternative or substitute available. In education, on the other hand, private education is of course counterbalanced and overshadowed by public education. Desegregation in public education presumably being a fact, an acceptable alternative is available. The reasonable educational goals of the Negro thus are fulfilled by integrated public education plus that part of private education that

53. Sutherland, "The Supreme Court and Private Schools," 25 *Harvard Education Review* 127, 128 (1955).

voluntarily desegregates. Thus, finding state action to be involved in private education would tip the scales too much in the other direction.

In addition, extending the concept of state action to true private education would tend to jeopardize all types of private group activity; only the most compelling reasons would lead the Court to open that Pandora's box. And many of the virtues of private education are existent because it is private and not controlled, except in a tenuous manner, by the state. There are values to be preserved, both individual and societal, by a continuation of the present system of education.

Finally, it may be said that the well-known reluctance of the Supreme Court to rule on constitutional questions would tend to make it postpone a decision on the question, should it arise, as long as possible.

In sum, it can be stated with certainty that there is little or no chance of a successful assault from without on the doors of true private education in the foreseeable future. The "private school" plans of some Southern states, enacted in an attempt to avoid the impact of the Court's decision, are quite another matter; it is probable that they generally will be invalidated judicially when, or if, they are challenged.

ADDENDUM

Before leaving this subject, it should be noted that state legislation designed to open the doors of private education to all by imposing standards of nondiscrimination in admission would be undoubtedly upheld under an attack on federal constitutional grounds. Some Northern states, notably New York, in fact have such statutes; they have met no serious challenge. The possible argument that imposed admission standards would interfere with religious freedom would undoubtedly also fail. The principle that upholds state prescription of standards for parochial school education is easily broad enough to include admission practices.[54]

54. See Note, 64 *Harvard Law Review* 307 (1950).

CHAPTER FIVE

LIMITATIONS IN GRANTS AND GIFTS

ONE RESULT of the strong preference in American law for the institution of private property has been the fact that a property owner is allowed to control its use, not only during his lifetime, but also long after his death. Liberty of testation has been the rule, although there have been some limitations imposed in every state. These, however, do not alter the basic proposition of control by the "dead hand."[1] "In any civilized society, there is no escape from the dead hand. In a sense we live by it. Our literature, our art, our architecture, our science, our religion, all are built upon the achievements of dead men."[2] As much can be said of private education: to a large extent its livelihood, its economic viability, is dependent upon the income derived from gifts and endowments from men long dead. Even when the gifts are made *inter vivos*—during the donor's lifetime—usually they last until after his death. The fact that those who endow universities and other private schools often attach special conditions to their gifts gives rise to another set of legal problems with respect to racial discrimination and private education.

Dead hand control can and does create two general

1. See Simes, *Public Policy and the Dead Hand* ch. 1 (1955).
2. *Ibid.*, at 140.

problem areas for the private school administrator in the context of the present inquiry. First, it may be that some of the endowment funds or other assets of a school have been granted with the provision that the beneficial use is limited to "whites" or "Caucasians" or some other racial group. This problem is neatly posed by the litigation involving famed Girard College in Philadelphia. Second, the possibility exists that grants of land may have been made to a school on condition that the land would revert to the grantor or his heirs should it ever be used for Negroes or other nonwhites. Another recent case illustrates this problem: *Charlotte Park and Recreation Comm'n v. Barringer*,[3] a North Carolina case.

It is evident that both of these problems involve essentially the same question. However, there is enough difference in them to make separate discussion advisable. But some general statements, germane to both areas, should precede the particularized development.

First, it is of the essence of the power of an owner over his property that he may limit the beneficial use of it as narrowly as he wishes. Thus, he may create a trust in his will and limit the beneficiaries under the trust to as small a group of people as he desires; and he may grant property to another on condition that it be used for certain purposes only, and, if it is not so used, that it revert to the grantor or his heirs. Even when explicit provision is made for the exclusion of certain racial groups, e.g., the Negroes, from the beneficial use of trust funds or of property, the restrictions are not invalid per se.[4]

---

3. 242 N.C. 311, 88 S.E. 2d 114 (1955). The Supreme Court refused to review the decision. Leeper v. Charlotte Park and Recreation Comm'n, 350 U.S. 983 (1956).

4. See, generally, 3 Scott, *Trusts* ch. 11 (1939).

Next, attacks on the types of private discrimination involved in the exclusion of racial groups from the beneficial use of trust funds or property have thus far centered around attempts to find some tie to official government action in order to get the requisite "state action" necessary to trigger the Fourteenth Amendment. No frontal assault has yet been made on the limitations themselves as being invalid. Thus, in the Girard College litigation the argument was made that the trust is administered by an official body the Philadelphia Board of Directors of City Trusts, and that this is sufficient connection to government to constitute state action. And in the *Charlotte Park* case the attempt was made to establish the proposition that operation of the clause under which the granted property reverted to the grantor was state action within the doctrine of *Shelley v. Kraemer* (discussed in Chapter Four).

Third, it may be possible to suggest methods of attacking the restrictive clauses directly. There may, in other words, be chinks in the doctrine of freedom of testation so far as racial limitations are concerned. There are a few judicial statements leaning toward this end; these may be harbingers of the things to come. In other words, it is possible, albeit improbable, that the racial restrictive clause will be outlawed entirely from deeds and grants of property.

Finally, both problem areas raise two questions: (1) May a person excluded because of race from the benefits of a trust bring an action to have the trust opened up to include him? and (2) May the trustees of such a trust (or the grantees under a grant of property) refuse to carry out its terms, that is to say, may they ignore the racial restrictions, and when brought to account in court plead that enforcement of the restriction is precluded by the *Shelley v. Kraemer* doctrine?

Since our attention is focused on private education, we will limit the present discussion to the relevant aspects of charitable trusts for educational purposes and to grants of land or other property to private schools. (The *Girard* case involved a charitable trust, and the *Charlotte Park* case dealt with the grant of land to a city.) A charitable trust, it should be noted, differs from the ordinary private trust in that it need not have a definite beneficiary and may be created to exist in perpetuity; private trusts usually must have a definite beneficiary and cannot be so created as to exist forever.[5]

THE GIRARD COLLEGE LITIGATION[6]

Under the terms of a trust created in 1831 by Stephen Girard for the education of "poor white male orphans," Girard College was established in Philadelphia. The school is administered by the Philadelphia Board of Directors of City Trusts, the trustee, in accordance with a

---

5. Simes, *supra* note 1, ch. 5 has a good brief discussion of this. See also Scott, "Education and the Dead Hand," 34 *Harvard Law Review* 1 (1920).

6. In re Estate of Stephen Girard, decided April 29, 1957, by the United States Supreme Court. That Court overruled the opinion of three Pennsylvania courts. The Pennsylvania Supreme Court, in its opinion of November 12, 1956, 127 Atl. 2d 287, 2 *Race Relations Law Reporter* 68, upheld the lower state courts' decisions that the Girard Trust did not involve state action. But the United States Supreme Court did not agree.

The case has engendered great interest. Discussions may be found, among other places, in Cahn, "Jurisprudence," 31 *New York University Law Review* 182 (1956); in Gordon, "The Girard College Case: Desegregation and a Municipal Trust," 304 *Annals* 53 (March, 1956); in Notes, 56 *Columbia Law Review* 285 (1956), 104 *University of Pennsylvania Law Review* 547 (1956); and in *U.S. News and World Report*, May 10, 1957, p. 54.

state statute. The Board consists of the Mayor and President of the City Council, both ex-officio, and twelve other members appointed by judges of the Courts of Common Pleas of the county. Its operations are conducted autonomously, free from any control of the city or state save for the jurisdiction of the Orphans' Court of Philadelphia, which oversees the trust administration. The Girard Trust is today worth some $95 million, the income from which goes for the most part to the support of Girard College.

Negro orphans, otherwise fully qualified, being poor and male, applied for admission to the school but were rejected by the trustees because of their race. They then petitioned the Orphans' Court for a determination that they were eligible for admission to the school, arguing (1) that the terms of the trust should be conformed to present-day conditions, (2) that racial discrimination was against public policy, and (3) that administration of the trust by a city-appointed board constituted state action that was invalid under the equal protection clause of the Fourteenth Amendment. In a comprehensive opinion, Judge Bolger of the Orphans' Court rejected these arguments and upheld the trust in accordance with its terms. Affirmed by the entire Orphans' Court sitting *en banc*, and again affirmed by the Supreme Court of Pennsylvania, it was carried to the United States Supreme Court in an attempt to get the constitutional question settled. In a brief opinion rendered April 29, 1957, that Court reversed the Pennsylvania courts. The federal Court said in its unsigned opinion, to which there was no dissent: "The Board which operates Girard College is an agency of the State of Pennsylvania. Therefore even though the Board was acting as a trustee, its refusal to admit [the Negro applicants] ... to the college because they were Negroes was discrimination by the State. Such discrimination is forbidden by the Fourteenth Amendment."

On the merits, the case stands neatly poised in the hazy area separating private from official action—an area that affords full opportunity for judicial craftsmanship. The decision could have gone either way in the Orphans' Court, for the close connection of the trust and the trustees could easily have brought it within the ambit of state action. The reason given for not finding state action was that the activity of the city was "proprietary" and not "governmental" in nature. That came close to saying that if a city acts like a private individual, then it becomes in law a private individual and loses its character of a governmental entity. Just how this metamorphosis was supposed to take place was left unstated by the judges of the Orphans' Court. Also left unstated was any justification for making a dichotomy between proprietary and governmental functions in the field of constitutional interpretation.[7] The United States Supreme Court had little difficulty in rejecting that conclusion. However, although the tie to the state is close enough for the Court to have found state action, still the policy considerations that may have motivated the Court in such a case as *Terry v. Adams* (the *Jaybird Primary* case)[8] were not present in the *Girard* case. The deprivation involved at Girard College

---

7. Cf. Lawrence v. Hancock, 76 F. Supp. 1004 (S.D.W. Va., 1948) (equal protection clause held to apply to municipal corporation in exercise of proprietary function).

8. This case was discussed in Chapter Four.

is not nearly so significant or so great as the instances when a Negro is kept from voting or from obtaining a job. Readily available is desegregated public education. And making a compelling argument for the integration of *a* private school is far different from making one leading to the desegregation of *all* private schools.[9]

Public Policy and Racial Clauses

The fact that the Girard Trust was held to involve state action is of less interest to a private school administrator than the fact that an attempt was made to outlaw the racial clause as being contrary to public policy. Another facet of interest and importance was the attempted application of the doctrine of cy pres to the trust. These two aspects of the *Girard College* case merit development in some detail.

The position of the Negro applicants, so far as public policy and the racial restrictive clause were concerned, was that the clause conflicted with the present public policy of the city of Philadelphia, the state of Pennsylvania, and the United States. The argument was based on a series of statutes and municipal ordinances dealing with racial matters and uniformly indicating that the official statements of the three governments pointed ineluctably toward a

9. It should be noted that, even with the decision of the United States Supreme Court, it is not at all certain that Negro applicants will now be accepted at Girard College. It is entirely possible that legal action will be taken to substitute a private trustee for the Board of City Trusts in Philadelphia. If such a substitution were made, the administration of the Trust and College would no longer be "state action" subject to the Fourteenth Amendment. The fact that both Philadelphia city officials and the state Attorney General supported the United States Supreme Court decision, however, may well indicate that no attempt will be made to have the will changed. Negroes, thus, may be admitted to Girard College.

policy of nondiscrimination.[10] Recent cases dealing with racial segregation, the Charter of the United Nations, and various pronouncements of the President in addition to the platforms of the two principal political parties were all offered as evidence sufficient to establish that the national policy of the United States is against racial discrimination. Both City of Philadelphia officials and the Attorney General of Pennsylvania filed briefs not only in support of the Negroes' applications but also on the specific point that the racial clause violates the present public policy of the city and state.

Neither the hearing Judge (Judge Bolger) nor the full bench of the Orphans' Court, in reaching their separate but identical decisions, dealt with this argument.[11] This failure to act is entirely understandable, for the public policy argument leaves the court with a most difficult choice: either it could say that the public policy of Philadelphia and Pennsylvania and the United States was in favor of or indifferent to racial discrimination (scarcely possible today), or it could say that the public policy was against racial discrimination, and in so doing not only open Girard College to Negro orphans but also strike a body blow at all types of private acts of discrimination. A third choice, that of calling the argument irrelevant, was also theoretically available; however, it was scarcely tenable. The Orphans' Court chose, rather, to ignore the argument

10. Brief for Exceptants William Ashe Foust and Robert Felder, In Re: Estate of Stephen Girard, pp. 33-41 (1955).

11. The only mention in the two opinions is in Judge Bolger's opinion; he stated, after setting out the argument of the petitioners, that "having construed the applicable constitutional provisions, the pertinent acts of assembly and court decisions [it is decided], that the operation of this trust does not offend public policy as so determined." 1 *Race Relations Law Reporter* 325, 338 (1956).

and base the decisions on a finding that the trust was valid and that no state action was involved.

The question is thus left dangling, though it is ripe for decision. How long such a decision can be postponed is, of course, unknown. However, the law seems to be moving in the direction of the creation of a public policy that will make racial discriminations invalid per se. Not only may the various statutes in many states as well as in the federal government be pointed to, but also there exist treaties, including the UN Charter, and executive orders of both President Truman and President Eisenhower, in addition to those of President Roosevelt,[12] that serve to buttress the point. So far as the judiciary is concerned, the decisions are indeed scant that would serve to establish the policy. Some scattered opinions do exist. For example, in *Hurd v. Hodge*,[13] in which the Supreme Court refused to enforce a restrictive covenant in the District of Columbia the Court said:

... even in the absence of statute, there are other considerations which would indicate that enforcement of restrictive covenants ... is judicial action contrary to the public policy of the United States.... The power of the federal courts to enforce the terms of private agreements is at all times exercised subject to the restrictions and limitations of the public policy of the United States as manifested in the Constitution, treaties, federal statutes, and applicable legal precedents.

The California Supreme Court in 1944 stated that there was "a public policy against racial discrimination ... [and] that a statute [was unnecessary] to enforce such a policy

12. The executive orders establishing the Fair Employment Practices Commission and its successors is an example. See Ruchames, *Race, Jobs, and Politics* (1953) for an account of the history of the FEPC.
13. 334 U.S. 24 (1948).

where private rather than public action is involved."[14] And in *Clifton v. Puente*,[15] the Texas Court of Civil Appeals in 1948 invalidated a racial restrictive covenant. A Canadian case, *Re Drummond Wren*,[16] is a direct holding to the effect that a racial restrictive covenant is void for the reason that it is contrary to public policy.

The point to all of this, so far as our present inquiry is concerned, is that the clear import of recent occurrences throughout the United States (and the world itself) is that even private acts of racial discrimination are wrongful and cannot be sanctioned by law. It has importance to the trustee of any charitable trust that may confine its benefits to certain racial groups, and it has importance to the administrators of those private schools that are beneficiaries of charitable trusts.

The Doctrine of Cy Pres

A final argument advanced by the Negro applicants in the *Girard* case involved the attempted application of the equitable doctrine of cy pres to the case. The argument was stated in the following manner: The changed circumstances in public policy, constitutional law, education, and human relations prevent Stephen Girard's educational objectives from being achieved under the continuation of racial restriction. Both the hearing judge and the full Orphans' Court rejected this argument, the full court saying that "there is . . . no present failure of the purpose of the trust; a fortiori, there is no ground for

---

14. James v. Marinship Corp., 25 Cal. 2d 721, 740 (1944).
15. 218 S.W. 2d 272 (Texas Civil Appeals, 1948).
16. [1945] D.L.R. 674. The *Wren* case, however, may have been overruled or its effect vitiated. See Comment, 29 *Canadian Bar Review* 969 (1951).

application of the cy pres doctrine."[17] Neither did the United States Supreme Court in its decision find it necessary to rule on this aspect of the case. Even so, the issue is one of importance and one that will undoubtedly reach the Courts in future cases. Hence, it is desirable to discuss it briefly at this point.

Cy pres is a doctrine applied generally by courts of equity to save a trust from dissolution in those cases when the precise intention of the settlor cannot be carried out. When allowed, the trust is continued on operation "as near as possible" to the settlor's intention. The definition given by the *Restatement of Trusts* is frequently quoted:

> If property is given in trust to be applied to a particular charitable purpose, and it is or becomes impossible or impracticable or illegal to carry out the particular purpose, and if the settlor manifested a more general intention to devote the property to charitable purposes, the trust will not fail but the court will direct the application of the property to some charitable purpose which falls within the general charitable intention of the settlor.[18]

While there is no single uniformly recognized definition of the doctrine, it has been stated that all "would probably agree that the value of the rule lies in its ability to provide the flexibility necessary to accommodate perpetual or long-lasting gifts to the exigencies of new conditions."[19]

So far as established doctrine is concerned, the decision of the Pennsylvania courts in the *Girard* case seems to be in accord with the holdings of most courts, although there have been no precisely similar factual situations litigated

---

17. Estate of Stephen Girard. I *Race Relations Law Reporter* 340, 342 (1956).
18. *Restatement of Trusts* § 399 (1935). See Scott, *Trusts* § 399 (1939).
19. Fisch, *The Cy Pres Doctrine in the United States* 2 (1950).

heretofore.[20] The question turns on the definition to be given to the word "impracticable" in the *Restatement* version of the cy pres doctrine; certainly the Girard Trust has neither become impossible nor illegal.[21] Now of course what is or is not impracticable is a question not susceptible to solution by mathematical formula; the answer will vary with the facts and circumstances of each case. The novel factual situation in the *Girard* case gave the Pennsylvania judiciary an opportunity to extend the cy pres doctrine. Should a new twist to that doctrine have been created?

Varying answers will, of course, be given to a question such as that. On the one hand, there is the position of the Orphans' Court: that application of the cy pres doctrine "would not only subvert the purpose of [Girard's] will, but would threaten, if not destroy, the entire structure of the law of wills in Pennsylvania."[22] This may be called the argument by logical extension to horrendous possibility. It is based on the assumption that there are no

20. See Fisch, *supra* note 19, *passim*.

21. Comment *m* of Section 399 of the *Restatement of Trusts* states: "If it is possible and practicable and legal to carry out the particular purpose designated by the settlor, the doctrine of cy pres is not applicable. In such case the court will compel the trustees to carry out the particular purpose even though in the opinion of the court a more useful disposition of the property might be made.

"Thus, if a testator bequeaths a sum of money for the establishment and maintenance of a school of engineering the court will not permit the application of the money to the erection and maintenance of a school of agriculture, merely because it appears that a school of agriculture would be more useful to the community.

"On the other hand, the doctrine of cy pres is applicable even though it is possible to carry out the particular purpose of the settlor, if to carry it out would fail to accomplish the general charitable intention of the settlor. In such a case it is 'impracticable' to carry out the particular purpose, in the broad sense in which that word is used in this Section. This is particularly likely to be the case where there has been a change of circumstances after the creation of the trust."

22. 1 *Race Relations Law Reporter* 340, 341 (1956).

restraints whatever on the disposition of property by will. As the Orphans' Court went on to say: "Jus desponendi is still cardinal and basic law." But of course there are limits on the power of testamentary disposition, and the true question is not as stated by the Orphans' Court but rather whether this is an appropriate time to engraft another limitation on the power of the dead hand to control present use of property. As Justice Frankfurter pointed out in another context, it serves no useful purpose in the decision of cases to "[conjure] up horrible possibilities that never happen in the real world." There is, in other words, no reason to think that modifying Girard's will today would result in the destruction of the entire structure of the law of wills.

On the other hand, it is argued that the exigencies of mid-twentieth century America make it incumbent that a policy of racial nondiscrimination be adhered to at least officially, that the effects of discrimination are so invidious as to harm both those who are its object and those who impose it, and that the general purposes of Girard's trust cannot be carried out in an institution that practices racial exclusion. Implicit in this argument is the view that all types of racial discrimination, both public and private, are improper per se, and the notion that traditional doctrines of private property must give way when a sufficient social reason exists. When viewed in this light, it can be said that the *Girard* case did have implications beyond the immediate issue before the Pennsylvania courts. Modifying Girard's will through the requested use of cy pres would have made a major change in law.

The question, in essence, is really one of policy—of

what is good social policy in the middle of the twentieth century—and not one of technical legal doctrine. For no matter how much a decision is cloaked with legal language showing ostensible adherence to long-established precedent, the decision is in final analysis based on notions of what is good policy. Holmes said it many years ago:

> The life of the law has not been logic: it has been experience. The felt necessities of the time, the prevalent moral and political theories, intuitions of public policy, avowed or unconscious, even the prejudices which judges share with their fellow-men, have had a good deal more to do than the syllogism in determining the rules by which men should be governed.[23]

The point is, it would appear, that the cy pres doctrine is available for use by a judge in the *Girard*-type of situation should he, for whatever reason, decide that the time was ripe for it.

Little or nothing exists as authority to help the judge in this decision. Perhaps some of the language of the *Restatement of Trusts* could be used, language that suggests a broad interpretation be given to the "impracticability" test for cy pres.[24] There is one English case, *In Re Dominion Students Hall Trust*,[25] that might be used since it bears striking similarity to the *Girard* factual situation. In that case, the court had under consideration a trust originally restricted to Dominion students of "European origin." A petition was filed to eliminate the color restriction. This was done, the court giving a narrow definition to the "impossibility" requirement of cy pres and a broad definition to "impracticability." It found that the

---

23. Holmes, *The Common Law* 1 (1881).
24. See *Restatement of Trusts* §§ 399, 381 (1945). See also 3 Scott, *Trusts* § 399 (1939).
25. [1947] 1 Ch. 183.

general purpose of the charity, promoting community of citizenship, culture, and tradition among all members of the British Commonwealth, far from being furthered by the color restriction, might in light of the changed times be defeated by creating antagonisms.[26]

If the decision in *Girard* was ultimately one of policy, then we can go a step farther and say that in final analysis the policy argument becomes, in part, one of deciding how much credence to give to the opinion of social scientists and others on the socio-psychological effect of patterns of discrimination. It is widely felt—probably erroneously—that the opinions of social scientists had persuasive effect in the decision of the Supreme Court in the *Segregation Cases*. Whether they did or not, it is worth noting that another attempt was made in the *Girard* litigation to use sociological and psychological data in an effort to prove that racial segregation had a deleterious effect, not on the Negroes excluded from attendance at Girard College, but on the white students there who were being deprived of the opportunity to mix with colored colleagues.

The argument ran as follows: Girard's will calls for the establishment of an institution to provide "for such a number of poor male white orphan children, as can be trained in one institution, a better education . . . than they

26. Judge Bolger, the hearing judge in the *Girard* case, discussed the English case in the following manner: "There a trust established and maintained by several contributors was restricted to dominion students 'of European origin.' The court eliminated a racial restriction because the retention of it would have caused a failure of the main purpose of the trust which was to benefit the empire. However, the change was made upon application by or with the approval of the contributors; the court pointing out that had the trust been established under a will, its power to make the change would have been at least doubtful." I *Race Relations Law Reporter* 325, 339 (1956).

usually receive from the application of public funds"; that they be taught "by every proper means a pure attachment to our republican institutions"; that they have instilled into their minds "the purest principles of morality so that on their entrance into active life they may, from inclination and habit, evince benevolence towards their fellow creatures. . . ." Testimony of several social scientists—a sociologist, an educator and psychologist, and a psychologist—was introduced; they were unanimously of the opinion that the experience of living in a segregated institutional community creates serious conflicts in the mind of the young student who is taught one thing and lives another. This testimony was counteracted by testimony of officers and former students of Girard College, who were of the opinion that no such deleterious effects resulted from racial exclusion.

The conflict in testimony was resolved by both the hearing judge and the full Orphans' Court on review by summarily dismissing the argument as irrelevant. "This testimony," the full court said, "does not affect the legal principles here involved."[27]

The enormously important question of what use should be made of socio-psychological data in the judicial decision-making process is one that is beyond the scope of this inquiry. It is, however, suggested that the manner in which the court handled that testimony was eminently correct. There are at least two reasons for this: First of all, present-day social science is far from being "scientific"; its propositions are based on what often is at best inconclusive evidence and are nothing more than tentative hy-

---

27. 1 *Race Relations Law Reporter* 340, 342 (1956).

potheses.[28] Secondly, even if the "scientific" propositions of our social scientists are verifiable and have validity, it is questionable that they have relevance; more, it is doubtful that they *should* be used for more than the limited purpose of indicating a factual basis for legislation. That was what the so-called "Brandeis Brief" sought to do: provide nonlegal data to indicate that legislative action was reasonable. But to use nonlegal data—the testimony of sociologists and psychologists and the like—for the purpose of overturning legislative action or declaring patterns of racial discrimination unconstitutional is quite another matter. Expert testimony of any type undoubtedly at times has value, but if we are not to turn law courts into forums for balancing the conflicting claims of various kinds of experts, then we should be extremely careful about admitting such testimony, and, if it is admitted into evidence, we should be extremely careful to insure that it is not given overriding importance. At best it would be but one factor among the many that any judge must consider in reaching a judicial decision.[29]

28. See Cahn, "Jurisprudence," 30 *New York University Law Review* 150 (1955); 31 *New York University Law Review* 182 (1956); Judge Jerome Frank's contribution to the symposium entitled "The Lawyer's Role in Modern Society: A Round Table," 4 *Journal of Public Law* 1, 8 (1955). But see, for a statement of the usefulness of social science data in judicial decision-making, Greenberg, "Social Scientists Take the Stand: A Review and Appraisal of Their Testimony in Litigation," 54 *Michigan Law Review* 953 (1956).

29. Despite the oft-repeated statement to the contrary, facts do not "speak for themselves." Still necessary, no matter how voluminous the accumulation of factual data may be, is a judgment upon those facts, a mental effort which cannot be escaped. There is, in the context of race relations, little or no dispute over the *facts* of discrimination or of the existence of, to use the language of Chief Justice Warren, "a feeling of inferiority" that segregation engenders; all, white or black, Northerner or Southerner, would agree. The lack of agreement is on what judgment should be placed on those facts—an entirely different matter. Or what the legal result of those facts should be—still different. This act of judgment

An Appraisal and a Question

The *Girard* case has important implications for the private school administrator. It may provide the springboard for an assault on the legal validity of racial restrictive clauses. For those institutions that have funds so earmarked, this would be particularly important. For all private institutions, denominational or otherwise, it could mean the beginning of an attempt to remove racial barriers to admission. Finally, there is left unasked in the discussion of the case a question that is important and should be raised. That question is: Suppose a trustee or school administrator decided not to await such possible developments, and suppose that, in direct violation of the terms of a trust or other grant of funds, it is decided to make the beneficial use of the funds available to Negroes —what would be the result?

The question is not easily answered. On the one hand, it is obvious that a trustee of trust funds who violates the terms of the trust may be removed and otherwise disciplined by the judiciary.[30] But that would mean the intervention of the state and resultant state action in what would, in essence, be the enforcement of a racial restriction. Under the Supreme Court decisions in *Shelley v. Kraemer* and *Barrows v. Jackson* (discussed in Chapter

---

is a profound, complex matter. Those who propose the use of social science data in racial cases presuppose the judgment to be rendered.

Furthermore, facts are not the easily ascertainable creatures they are usually considered to be. Rather, just what the facts of any given situation may be is an inquiry that at best is fraught with uncertainty. We assume, for example, that a jury finds the facts in a trial; but that is scarcely true. At best, the jury finds what it considers to be the facts, and it is obvious that its view of the facts may be widely at variance with what actually took place. Cf. Frank, *Courts on Trial* 211-12 (1950); Easton, "Shifting Images of Social Science and Values," 15 *Antioch Review* 3 (1955).

30. See, e.g., 3 Bogert, *Trusts and Trustees* § 527 (1946).

Four) judicial enforcement of a racial clause is a denial of equal protection of the laws and thus unconstitutional. Does this mean that a trustee may safely ignore a racial clause?

The question asks too much for answer here. It will have to suffice merely to raise it and to forego attempting an extended discussion. One thing, however, is clear and should be mentioned: The recent court decisions on racial matters, when added to other official pronouncements in the area, have importance beyond the immediate context in which they are made; there is no doubt that they will have important effects in many areas of what has traditionally been called "private law," including the law of contracts, of trusts, and of property.[31]

THE BARRINGER CASE[32]

In 1955 the North Carolina Supreme Court rendered a decision which has importance to our present inquiry. The case was *Charlotte Park & Recreation Comm'n v. Barringer*, involving a grant of property with the proviso that the beneficial use of the property be limited to members of the white race. The facts are these: In 1929 Barringer conveyed land to a public corporation in Charlotte, North Carolina, for use as a municipal park, with the limitation that "in the event that the said land . . . shall not be kept, used and maintained for park, playground, and/or recreational purposes, for use by the white race only, and if such disuse or nonmaintenance continue for any period

---

31. Cf. Huber, "Revolution in Private Law?" 6 *South Carolina Law Quarterly* 8 (1953).

32. Charlotte Park and Recreation Comm'n v. Barringer, 242 N.C. 311, 88, S.E. 2d 114 (1955). Of the several comments on this case in legal periodicals, see especially Note, 34 *North Carolina Law Review* 113 (1955).

as long as one year, ... then ... the lands hereby conveyed shall revert in fee simple to the [grantor]."

The North Carolina court construed this limitation to be a valid fee simple determinable, which would revert automatically, without the intervention of the state judiciary, should Negroes use the land. "The determinable fee ... automatically will cease and terminate by its own limitation expressed in the deed, and estate granted automatically will revert [to the grantor], by virtue of the limitation in the deed." *Shelley v. Kraemer*, the restrictive covenant case, was held to have no application.

As with the *Girard* case, so it is with the *Barringer* case: there is relevance and importance to our inquiry. The technicalities of property law need not overly concern us. Whether the court was technically accurate in terming the racial clause a fee simple determinable may be of interest to property lawyers, but is not germane here; there is no doubt that a clause that would operate automatically could easily be drafted by anyone knowledgeable in the field.

Whether one agrees with the North Carolina court or not, it stands as law in that state, for the United States Supreme Court has refused to review the decision.[33] Even so, there are some important questions left dangling by the North Carolina court. Why was the racial condition not void as being contrary to law and public policy? And since the title to the land reverted to the grantor "by operation of law," that is, by operation of the common law of North Carolina, why is that not state action within the

---

33. The case name was changed in the Supreme Court decision to Leeper v. Charlotte Park and Recreation Comm'n, 350 U.S. 983 (1956). As is usual, the Court gave no reason for denying certiorari.

rule of *Shelley v. Kraemer?* Finally, assuming that a grantee would refuse to give up possession of the property, would an action of ejectment by the grantor involve invalid state action?

It would have done no violence to widely accepted legal doctrine had the North Carolina court declared the condition void and refused to enforce it. A limitation on an estate conveyed is often considered to be invalid and unenforceable if it is contrary to law or established public policy. An illustration is the case of *Trustees of Eureka College v. Bondurant*,[34] involving a conveyance of land to a college on condition that the land would revert to the grantor if the receipts therefrom were not used in a certain manner. The Illinois Supreme Court found that the condition was in conflict with a provision in the college charter and held the condition void. In the *Barringer* case, the conduct required by the grantee of the land to carry out the condition is unlawful under present-day law: the Commission would have had to exclude Negroes from a municipal golf course. Such exclusion is unlawful since the decisions by the United States Supreme Court in late 1955 in the *Holmes* and *Dawson* cases.[35] It is of course true that *Barringer* was decided before *Holmes* and *Dawson*; thus, in a technical sense the law had not yet been established. Nevertheless, it was clearly foreseeable; furthermore, there is no doubt that racial discrimination by a public body in the use of public facilities is against national public policy.

34. 289 Ill. 289, 124 N.E. 652 (1919).
35. Holmes v. Atlanta, 350 U.S. 879 (1955) (held a denial of equal protection to exclude Negroes from municipally owned golf course); Baltimore v. Dawson, 350 U.S. 877 (1955) (unconstitutional to deny Negroes access to public bathing beaches).

All of which makes the denial of certiorari by the United States Supreme Court inexplicable. In so doing it left standing a case that bids fair to undercut the effectiveness of the *Shelley v. Kraemer* doctrine and cries out for authoritative decision. Of course, the Court has discretion in such matters; it can review or not as it wishes. But even so, the Court does have a responsibility to render decisions on constitutional questions, a responsibility that should not be lightly shrugged off. Having assumed the power of decision, and having exercised it for more than 150 years, the Court is hardly fulfilling its high judicial purpose when it leaves the type of question raised in the *Barringer* case unresolved.[36]

As with the question of the validity of the reverter clause itself, so it is with the second question left unanswered by the *Barringer* case. It would do no violence to accepted methods and notions for the North Carolina court to have found state action in the fact that "by opera-

---

36. The Court moves in mysterious ways its wonders to perform: it will refuse to review a case and leave the decision below standing while at the same time stoutly maintaining that its decision is not to be construed as indicative of its feeling on the issues of the case denied review. But of course the Court is relatively alone on that position; in the mind of the general public at least, and perhaps generally throughout the bar, a denial of certiorari is given more weight.

But it is a fairly general practice. One reason for the refusal to review the *Barringer* decision may be that members of the Court feel that they have gone about as far as is feasible at this time in altering the legal pattern in racial relations. The school cases and the recreation cases taken together make a large mouthful for the South to chew and swallow. In going that far, the Court took what may certainly be thought of as a calculated risk. The reaction generated in the South may have been enough for the Court to steer clear of further acerbity of conditions. This could serve to explain, partially at least, the Courts' action in the *Barringer* case as well as its seizing upon the weakest and flimsiest of reasons to refuse to make a decision in the Virginia miscegenation case. See Naim v. Naim, 350 U.S. 891 (1955). A subsequent opinion of the Supreme Court of Appeals in the *Naim* case may be found at I *Race Relations Law Reporter* 404 (1956).

tion of law" title to the land would revest in the grantor. Such a finding would be an extension of the state action doctrine of the *Shelley* and *Barrows* cases, but it is a logical one—perhaps the next logical one. For law, despite never-ending arguments over definitions, exists only when the full force of society acting through government is behind it. As was said by Justice Brandeis, "law in the sense in which the courts speak of it today does not exist without some definite authority behind it. The common law so far as it is enforced in a state ... [is] the law of that state existing by authority of that state."[37] The reverter clause in *Barringer* did operate "automatically," as the North Carolina court maintained, but that was true only because North Carolina law (with the full force of the state behind it) allowed it to do so.[38]

The third question left dangling by the North Carolina court is basically similar to those already discussed. That question is: Would an action of ejectment, brought by the

37. Erie Railroad Co. v. Tompkins, 304 U.S. 64, 79 (1938).
38. However, it is clear that if this line of argument is followed and accepted, then it would be difficult to see what activities would fail to be state action. For example, a country club limiting its membership on racial grounds gains its status through the operation of the law in which it exists. If it is state action for the automatic operation of a fee simple determinable, then why would it not be equally state action when a state agency incorporated the country club? The principle seems to be the same in both cases. What, then, is the end? Once the concept of state action is pushed beyond the usual activities of state organs into situations usually considered to be private or nonofficial, then it would seem that there would be no limit to what could be called state action. Some have suggested that the Fourteenth Amendment was designed to eliminate individual acts of discrimination (see Flack, *Adoption of the Fourteenth Amendment* 262-63 [1908]), but the Supreme Court has never so held.

In the final analysis, what is state action depends—as in all constitutional questions—upon what the Supreme Court says it is. And what the Court says is, as usual, based in turn upon notions of what good public policy should be at the time the decision is rendered. There exist no table of logarithms, no formula, no vade mecum by which this decision may be made.

holder of the reversionary interest against a recalcitrant grantee who refused to give up the property, involve state action within the scope of the doctrine of *Shelley v. Kraemer?* While this question could be decided by a court using conceptualistic reasoning—that is, stating that the court would not be enforcing the racial condition but merely removing a person whose right to possession had terminated automatically upon breach of the condition—the result would be that the racial clause would be enforced by indirection. As the Texas Court of Civil Appeals said in *Clifton v. Puente*,[39] it is as much state action to "deny to a person a legal right to which he would be entitled except for the covenant as it would be to expressly command by judicial order that the terms of the covenant be recognized and carried out." The same sort of reasoning would apply in the converse situation: suppose the reversioner got possession in some manner and the grantee sought to eject him, with the reversioner setting up "title" through automatic reversion as a defense. Conceptualistically, this could provide a basis for decision. But again, the true nature and the practical result would be the same: indirect enforcement of a racial clause that admittedly could not be directly enforced.

What a court would do in such a situation depends in part on the extent to which it would be willing to pierce the form of a situation and get to the substance. In other words, the question would be whether the court would be willing to cut through to the core and recognize the practical results of a decision. Whether it would or not depends, in final analysis, not on a judge's view of what

39. 218 S.W. 2d 272 (Texas Civil Appeals, 1948).

"the law" is, for here the judge must choose between competing statements of law. Rather, it depends upon subjective views of what the individual judicial decision-maker believes is desirable or acceptable social policy in the world as it is today.[40]

AN EVALUATION

We may be moving into an entire new era in the field of racial relations. At a time when the Negro and other minority groups are battling to attain formal equality in treatment from official bodies—and certainly that battle is far from won, although significant strides have been made—there seems to be a parallel movement developing. Perhaps by inadvertence, perhaps by design, there are definite indications that more than the absence of official governmental acts of discrimination is wanted. Of course, the Negro wants "first class citizenship" with full voting rights and an opportunity to enjoy fully the facilities— recreational, educational, and the like—that his taxes help pay for. But he wants, and is demanding, more: full and free opportunity for employment, for one thing. The

40. This statement does not, of course, coincide with what Morris R. Cohen called the "phonograph" theory of justice and what others have called the "slot machine" theory of the judicial process. Those theories, long exploded but still hanging tenaciously on, are bottomed on the view that a judge has no creative role in making a decision, but merely applies known law to the facts in a mechanical fashion; the job of the judge is to find the law—after that the result is preordained. This naïve notion is part of the basic theory that ours is a government "of laws, not of men." A present-day variation is the hue and cry from Southern spokesmen that the Supreme Court engaged in "judicial legislation" in the *Segregation Cases*. The simple truth of the matter is that the judiciary have always "legislated," that is to say, have always been policy-makers. The common law itself is a product of this process. A judge cannot avoid making policy—"legislating"—when he renders a decision. See Cahill, *Judicial Legislation* (1952); Cardozo, *The Nature of the Judicial Process* (1921); Levi, *An Introduction to Legal Reasoning* (1949).

parallel movement, thus, is one which is aimed at crumbling the walls of racial discrimination in activities and institutions long considered to be entirely within the domain of "private" action.

Seen in this light, the action brought by the Negro applicants to gain entry into Girard College takes on added significance. It could well be the opening gun in a battle to breach the walls of private education. At the very least, it attempts to add another large segment to the expanding net of state action. Hence, the case has importance to the private school administrator for two reasons: one is that just stated—it is possibly the opening attack on the admission policies of private schools; the other is that the possible ultimate outcome of such actions will be the elimination of racial clauses in trusts and grants of funds or property either through the judicial recognition of a public policy against such clauses or through the judicial outlawing of such clauses.

Whether either one of these possibilities will take place is pure speculation. But it is not so speculative to say that the demands being made by the colored ten percent of the American population are aimed at more than the elimination of official discriminations. That being so, it is possible to forecast that a continued use of law and the American legal machinery will be made as the Negro continues his efforts to gain full status in the American social structure.

CHAPTER SIX

AN APPRAISAL

IN THE FOREGOING chapters we have discussed the legal problems inherent in any attempt of a private school to admit both Negroes and whites to its student body. A number of conclusions, most of them admittedly tentative, have been drawn; others may now be added.

Before doing so, it is important to point out that the problems discussed are but one facet of the over-all question of Negro-white relations in the United States and of the changes which will be made in existing patterns of practice in those relations. An understanding of the aspirations of the Negro citizens, together with insight into the fears of the white citizens about the Negroes, would seem to be indispensable to an understanding of Negro-white relations now and in the future. The legal problems involved, whether in education or elsewhere, spring after all out of the greater milieu and are to be understood only as a part of that context. A valid view of the problem of racial integration of the private schools has to include insight into the over-all pattern.

But it is precisely there that we do not have that exact knowledge of factual conditions that is a prerequisite to understanding. We do not know, save in the broadest of generalities, and then only from a few spokesmen, what the Negroes actually want; we do not know, except for certain emotion-packed statements, what it is that the white man fears and dislikes about close association with the Negro. The thrust of race relations, if not of all society, is manifestly toward the creation of conditions of equality. In the past one hundred years the Negro has vaulted from slavery to a position of being able to insure equality of treatment from governmental officials. Possibly, the dynamics of the Negro movement will allow the Negro to stop when the goal of equality under the law has full operational reality as well as reality in the statements of courts and legislatures—at such time, that is, that the Negro is in fact accorded full access to all public privileges or services. Possibly, however, the movement will continue until the Negro reaches that equality of conditions that de Tocqueville thought was the unique feature of the United States; for, as de Tocqueville also said, equality in several areas of life will ineluctably result in equality in all: "To conceive of men remaining forever unequal upon one single point, yet equal in all others, is impossible; they must come in the end to be equal upon all."

The demands being made by the Negro, the demands he will be making in the future, the reaction that the white man and society generally makes to those demands—all of this we do not know. And not knowing it, any conclusions we have drawn or may draw from the present study can be based only upon incomplete evidence and upon those trends that are presently discernible. For the dynamics of the Negro movement will unavoidably color and influence the conditions under which all education will operate. With that limitation in mind, what can be said about the intermixture of the races in denominational and other private schools?

1. As a beginning, we can state that opposition, whether of governmental official or private individual, to a private school integrating the races will vary in relation to the incidence of Negroes to whites in the geographical area in which the school operates, and, in addition, will vary in direct proportion to the number of Negroes who are admitted to a former all-white school (regardless of geographical area). The first half of this statement is obvious from what has transpired since the May, 1954, decision in the public school segregation cases: the greatest opposition to the decision has come from the areas where the Negroes are thickest population-wise. The second half is not so obvious, but nevertheless valid. When it is seen that the white students in any public school will far outnumber the colored, then the opposition is slight at most and easily overcome. The same thing can be said about a private school. No problem that cannot be easily handled arises anywhere if the private school admits one or even several Negroes: this has happened often at all levels of education and in some of the most highly regarded private schools in the country. But it would be quite another matter for any school to admit one hundred Negroes or, say, twenty or thirty percent of its student body. It is doubtful indeed, should such an unlikely event take place, that it would be accomplished without incident. And geography would have nothing to do with the matter.

The point is this: Any institution or group (e.g., a fraternity or sorority) can easily assimilate into its ranks one or even a few who do not fully conform to the usual characteristics of its members. The group can even take pride in or gain satisfaction from such an "enlightened" policy. But what would happen if the institution or group was faced with the possibility that half its membership were to be "strange" or "nonconforming"? The conclusion must be that there would be strong opposition not only from the "ins" of the group but also from those outside (alumni, donors, etc.) who feel closely identified with it or are otherwise affected or influenced by it. Racial integration in the private schools of the North, through which a handful of Negroes are admitted to schools formerly denied to them, proves nothing so far as the creation of a model for other schools is concerned.

2. In those sections of the South where the incidence of colored to white is greatest—in the so-called "black belt"—any publicized decision by a private school administration to integrate would probably be met by strong opposition. This hostility would be from official (governmental) and nonofficial (private) sources.

Publicity would seem to be the key here, plus the number of schools involved. An individual private school, operating quietly and without fanfare, could probably admit Negroes and suffer few, if any, adverse consequences. Evidence of this may be found in the examples of Spring Hill College in Mobile, Alabama, Columbia Theological Seminary in Decatur, Georgia, Vanderbilt University in Nashville, Tennessee, and Loyola University in New Orleans, Louisiana. Although these examples are at the university level where it has been demonstrated that the least opposition is made to racial integration, the integration was done quietly and without public announcement. Compare this with the furor raised when Archbishop Rummel announced the decision to integrate the parochial schools of Louisiana: the publicity (plus the number of schools involved) caused an immediate fierce reaction.

Lack of publicity means a concomitant lack of wide public knowledge and the opportunity for public officials to ignore the occurrence. The officials can close their eyes, even when the integration means the violation of state law. No one is putting pressure upon them. Accordingly, they are not forced to make a decision. Let, however, the integration become widely publicized, let it have the cognizance of the mass of the people, and it is likely that the officials would have to make a decision. When that time comes, the result is entirely predictable: the officials would be forced to take action to uphold the statute or, in any event, to oppose the integration policy. To a large extent, it can be said that what took place in the over-publicized Autherine Lucy incident at the University of Alabama is an illustration of this point.

3. Mentioned in Chapter Two has been the fact that in some of the states, notably Kentucky, Tennessee, and Oklahoma which have statutory provisions designed to prevent integration of private schools, a number of institutions of higher learning have announced and put into effect integration policies without adverse reaction. Just why this challenge to state law has been allowed to go on without official objection is a question for which there is no ready answer. Whether it will be allowed to continue unhampered in like fashion cannot be answered. Should, however, governmental sanctions be invoked at some time

against an integrating school and its administration, it is likely that the sanctions would eventually be found to be invalid under the Constitution. The reach of the due process and equal protection clauses of the Fourteenth Amendment appears to be great enough to proscribe both affirmative acts of discrimination by state governments and governmental actions designed to make individuals follow discriminatory practices. The Constitution, in other words, not only means that governments must be color-blind but, further, that governments cannot require individuals to make color distinctions.

4. It would, however, be far more difficult to get a judicial decision of invalidation should the state outwardly comply with a policy of nondiscrimination but administratively make distinctions so that law is in fact applied with an uneven hand. The difficulties relate to proof and not to the principle involved. The law would be clear; it might be somewhat of a burden to prove violations.

Should a law enforcement official seek to bring the state's police power against an integrating private school by enforcing strictly a safety or sanitary or other such regulation, in all probability this would be found to be almost impossible to combat judicially. It is a breakdown of the democratic system for such occurrences to take place, but there is nothing in the Constitution to prevent such action. The lengths to which officials could go would be limited only by their imagination and perhaps their consciences.

5. It is in the area of unofficial sanctions privately imposed that the school could suffer the most severe deprivations. Physically, economically, psychologically,

the techniques of social control that could be brought to bear would transcend those that the state could bring to bear officially. The school administrators, faculty, and students, all could feel the full weight of social pressures exerted by other members of the status groups in which they live. These sanctions are in the realm of private action that could not, under any tenable theory, be brought within the reach of law.

6. If it is true that the dynamics of the Negro movement will include efforts to breach the walls of separation and discrimination in whatever form they take and whereever located, then it is possible that an attempt will be made to have racial admission barriers in private education lowered by court action. In one sense, this would be the next logical step for the flow of doctrine to take; it is a step that could be taken without doing too much damage to existing concepts and principles. But in this area and, for that matter, in other areas of constitutional interpretation, logic plays at best a minor role. It is unlikely that a court would take the step, now or in the foreseeable future.

7. Nevertheless, it can be forecast with some certainty that efforts will be made to have racial clauses in private agreements outlawed as a matter of public policy. The decisions in recent years have been edging toward that end. In fact, it can be said that the purport of recent decisions in racial cases has been to make the racial clause in effect a dead letter.

8. The denominational school would, as a general rule, be treated in the same manner as other private schools. The religious-freedom argument based upon the First

Amendment would probably not be enough to convince the Supreme Court that parochial schools should be treated differently.

9. Finally, it may well be that racial integration in the denominational and other private schools will be the wedge that opens the doors of the public schools in many parts of the South. If the pattern already started in an increasing number of private institutions of desegregating their student bodies continues, then the private school may operate as a proving ground for testing racial relations in education. Assuming some comparatively high degree of success in private school integration, the road ahead for the public schools may possibly be found. If the fears, rational or irrational, of the white man are not realized in one system of education, perhaps he will withdraw his opposition to integration in the other (public) school system.

Accordingly, what happens in the nonpublic schools in the South and elsewhere has an importance that transcends the school itself. As a testing ground for new patterns of racial relations, it could be the harbinger of things to come. Whether the future will include general racial integration or not may depend, to some large extent, upon the individuals now groping their way onto the unfamiliar ground of Negro-white educational commingling in the South.

TABLE OF CASES

INDEX

TABLE OF CASES

Baltimore v. Dawson, 117
Barney v. City of New York, 76
Barrows v. Jackson, 79, 80, 81, 114, 119
Berea College v. Kentucky, 14, 23, 24, 26, 42
Betts v. Easley, 85, 91
Bolling v. Sharpe, 3
Brotherhood of Railroad Trainmen v. Howard, 91
Brown v. Baskin, 85
Brown v. Board of Education, 3, 72 (See *Segregation Cases* in Index)

Cantwell v. Connecticut, 46-47
Charlotte Park & Recreation Comm'n v. Barringer, 80, 98 ff., 115 ff.
Civil Rights Cases, 75, 109
Clifton v. Puente, 106, 120
Cochran v. Board of Education, 27
Coulter v. Louisville & Nashville Ry., 41

Dominion Students Hall Trust, *In Re*, 110
Dorsey v. Stuyvesant Town Corporation, 85, 87-88
Drummond Wren, *Re*, 106

Erie Railroad v. Tompkins, 119
Everson v. Board of Education, 27, 46
Ex parte Virginia, 75

Fogg v. Board of Education, 11

Girard College case, 100 ff.
Grovey v. Townsend, 84

Holmes v. Atlanta, 117
Home Tel. & Tel. Co. v. Los Angeles, 75, 77
Hurd v. Hodge, 105

Iowa-Des Moines National Bank v. Bennett, 77-78

James v. Marinship Corporation, 91-92, 106

Kerr v. Enoch Pratt Free Library, 85-86

Lane v. Wilson, 83
Lawrence v. Hancock, 102

Marsh v. Alabama, 85, 88-89
Meyer v. Nebraska, 9, 14, 15, 18, 42-44
Minneapolis & St. Louis Ry. v. Beckwith, 41

Naim v. Naim, 118
Nixon v. Condon, 84, 86
Nixon v. Herndon, 83
Norris v. Mayor & City of Baltimore, 85, 87

People v. Stanley, 16
Pierce v. Society of Sisters, 9, 11, 13, 14, 18, 21, 42-44

Raymond v. Chicago Union Traction Co., 75, 77

Reynolds v. United States, 47
Rice v. Elmore, 84
School District v. Alamance County, 72
Screws v. United States, 78
Shelley v. Kraemer, 78-80, 99, 100, 114, 116, 118-20
Sioux City Bridge Co. v. Dakota County, 41
Slaughterhouse Cases, 74
Smith v. Allwright, 84, 86, 87
Snowden v. Hughes, 41
Steele v. Louisville & Nashville Ry., 90

Sunday Lake Iron Co. v. Wakefield, 41
Syres v. Oil Workers International Union, 90, 92

Terry v. Adams, 85, 102
Trustees of Dartmouth College v. Woodward, 14
Trustees of Eureka College v. Bondurant, 117

Virginia v. Rives, 76

Yick Wo v. Hopkins, 41

INDEX

Alabama, 35, 37, 60

Barry College, 49
Berea College, 23

Carter, Hodding, 59
Cash, John, 57
Columbia Theological Seminary 49, 126
Corwin, Edward R., 40, 43

Due process of law, 42 ff.

Education, theory of, 12; social need for, 12, 13, 72

First Amendment, 26, 30, 38, 46-47
Fifteenth Amendment, 83 ff.
Florida, 34
Fourteenth Amendment, 16, 20, 23, 26, 30-31, 33, 38, 39, 45, 73-74, 81-82

Georgia, 29-30

Interposition, 25

Jim Crowism, 56
Judicial legislation, 121

Kentucky, 34, 126
Ku Klux Klan, 36, 57-58

Laws requiring segregation, 24 ff.
Limitations in grants and gifts, 100 ff.; under cy pres doctrine, 106 ff.; Girard College case, 100 ff.

Louisiana, 25, 31, 36, 45, 127
Loyola University, 126
Lucy, Autherine, 36, 60, 127

Mississippi, 25, 31, 49, 61

N.A.A.C.P., 33, 35-36, 53, 61, 63
Negroes, vii, 38, 55, 56, 67, 83, 92; aspirations of, 69 ff., 121-22; voting, 82 ff.
North Carolina, 66

Oklahoma, 34, 66, 126

Pound, Roscoe, 51
Private schools, compared to public, 6-7; control by state, 14-17; enrollment, 6-8; income, 8; legal status, 8-13; place of, 4 ff.; those racially integrated, 38n; state authority over, 14-17; tax exemptions for, 27-30.
"Private-school plans," ix, 4, 25, 51, 53, 95

Roman Catholic church, 10, 11, 22, 25, 65
"Rule of Law," 34

Sanctions against racial integration, 21 ff.; governmentally imposed, 24-50; privately imposed, 51-67.
Segregation Cases, vii, 3, 19, 24, 39, 42, 52-53, 68, 71-72, 93, 111
Social control, 51
Social-science data, use of in judicial decisions, 112-13

South Carolina, 49, 58, 84
Spring Hill College, 49, 126
"State action" under the Constitution, 72 ff.

Taft, Senator Robert, 5
Tennessee, 33-34, 126

Tenth Amendment, 26
Thirteenth Amendment, 82

Vanderbilt University, 49, 126

White Citizens Councils, 58-59, 62
Woodward, C. Vann, 56

www.ingramcontent.com/pod-product-compliance
Lightning Source LLC
Chambersburg PA
CBHW030115010526
44116CB00005B/255